RICHARD B. LILLICH is Director of the International Legal Studies program in the College of Law, Syracuse University. He has specialized in international law as student, teacher, and practitioner. Educated at Oberlin, Cornell, and New York University, where he earned the degree of Doctor of Juridical Science, he also attended the Hague Academy of International Law. He is a member of the New York Bar.

GORDON A. CHRISTENSON is Attorney-Adviser (International) in the Office of the Legal Adviser, U.S. Department of State, handling legal problems for the Bureaus of Near-Eastern and South-Asian Affairs. He was formerly responsible at the working level for international claims involving Europe, the U.S.S.R., Turkey, Iceland, and other countries. A graduate of the University of Utah, Mr. Christenson holds the degree of Doctor of Juridical Science from The George Washington University and is a member of the Utah Bar.

INTERNATIONAL CLAIMS:

Their Preparation and Presentation

INTERNATIONAL CLAIMS:

Their Preparation and Presentation

Richard B. Lillich

Gordon A. Christenson

SYRACUSE UNIVERSITY PRESS

1962

MANUFACTURED IN THE UNITED STATES OF AMERICA

BY THE VAIL-BALLOU PRESS, INC., BINGHAMTON, NEW YORK

To

MEREDITH AND KATHERINE

Preface

THIS book is the outgrowth of one author's study of national claims commissions and the other author's experience in handling international claims for the Department of State. Several years ago it became apparent to us, as it had to many international lawyers, that no work existed that would aid the attorney for a claimant in preparing and presenting an international claim. The Department of State and the Foreign Claims Settlement Commission, while protesting the submission of ill-founded and ill-prepared claims, have been able to distribute, of necessity, only brief written suggestions to claimants and their attorneys. This book, the second volume in a series prepared under the auspices of Syracuse University College of Law's International Legal Studies Program and published by Syracuse University Press, is designed to fill this very real need.

The procedural side of international law, called by Feller "the Antarctica of international law," is seldom-explored territory. To help chart our course, we prepared and circulated to leading private and governmental lawyers several tentative outlines, and at a later date we profited from their observations on various drafts of portions of this book. If sins of omission or commission. exist, they are of course our responsibility, but we ask our readers to view them with whatever indulgence may be accorded to those who have attempted to blaze a trail.

Among those persons who have given us great assistance are George W. Spangler, Assistant Legal Adviser, and Edward G. Misey, Deputy Assistant Legal Adviser, Department of State; Donald E. Claudy, Esq. and Irving R. M. Panzer, Esq., of the District of Columbia Bar; Hon. Edward D. Re, Chairman, Foreign Claims Settlement Commission; Dr. Martin Domke and Dr. Ivan Soubbotitch of New York City; and Fabian A. Kwiatek, Attorney, Department of State. Professor Peter E. Herzog and Professor John Huston, colleagues on the Syracuse University College of Law faculty, have made significant contributions along the way.

Credit for the bibliography must go in large measure to Douglas E. Dayton, Esq., of the New York Bar, Lecturer on International Law at the New York University School of Law, who graciously gave us his permission to build upon the bibliography he had prepared for his course in International Claims. This bibliography was updated and supplemented through the efforts of Mr. John D. Elmer, Syracuse University College of Law Class of 1962 and 1962–1963 Africa-Asia Public Service Fellow. Donald L. Horowitz, Esq., of the New York Bar, rendered assistance in connection with the correction of proofs and the preparation of the index. Finally, our thanks are due the Editor-in-Chief of the Syracuse Law Review for his permission to use as Chapter VI of this book the substance of an article originally appearing in that review. We wish we had had a faithful typist to whom we now could extend thanks for typing the final manuscript.

For the record, the views expressed herein are solely those of the authors and do not necessarily represent the official opinion of the Department of State or the Foreign Claims Settlement Commission.

Richard B. Lillich
Gordon A. Christenson

Washington, D.C.
May, 1962

Contents

Introduction

THE law of international claims, sometimes called "the diplomatic protection of citizens abroad" or "the responsibility of states for injuries to aliens," is a subject of great interest to American lawyers, businessmen with foreign interests, and students of international law. While the latter may view the problem as another facet of the effort to subject the nations of the world to a rule of law by promoting the peaceful settlement of international disputes, the former two groups have a more mundane, bread-and-butter concern in the field. Since the end of World War II, at least one-third of a billion dollars has been disbursed to American claimants, both natural persons and business associations, in payment of international claims. Jessup aptly observes that "these claims settlements are not of particular interest to the student of power politics, but it is apparent from the sums of money involved, that they have been of interest to many practicing lawyers." [1]

[1] JESSUP, THE USE OF INTERNATIONAL LAW 99 (1959).

This interest is not likely to abate. At present claims against Czechoslovakia and Poland are being adjudicated by the Foreign Claims Settlement Commission of the United States,[2] while the Department of State, having concluded a lump sum settlement with Poland whereby over the next twenty years the Polish government will pay $40,000,000 to compensate American nationals for the nationalization of their property by Poland,[3] is attempting to negotiate a settlement with Czechoslovakia.[4] The adjudication of claims against Germany, hanging fire for over fifteen years, may soon be entrusted to the Commission. As one lawyer has noted, "the deluge of litigation which promises to descend on the Commission upon the enactment of a German Claims Act poses an exciting challenge to the alert practitioner."[5] Claims against Cuba for the taking of American property, while remaining unsettled at present, are being received by the Department of State for eventual action. Each week the Department considers many less spectacular, individual claims occasioned by the acts of foreign countries.

Moreover, the number of international claims seems destined to increase. Foreign trade and investment is at an all-time high. According to The New York Times, in 1960 "American industry's direct investment in other countries came to $30,000,-000,000, roughly three times as much as one decade earlier and mounting at a rate of more than $2,500,000,000 a year."[6] Over 2,800 United States corporations have a direct interest in one or

---

[2] FCSC, FOURTEENTH SEMIANN. REP. 1 (1961).

[3] Agreement With Poland, July 16, 1960 [1960] 11 U.S.T. & O.I.A. 1953, T.I.A.S. No. 4545. See Rode, *The American-Polish Claims Agreement of 1960*, 55 AM. J. INT'L L. 452 (1961).

[4] N.Y. Times, Oct. 27, 1961, p. 4, cols. 3–4.

[5] Goodman, *Claims Involving American Life and Property Abroad Under the Federal Foreign Claims Act*, 37 U. DET. L. J. 617, 623 (1960).

[6] N.Y. Times, June 25, 1961, § E, p. 5, col. 1.

more of 10,000 enterprises abroad.[7] Social and economic changes in some countries and chronic instability in others are bound to impair this investment and generate many claims. Trade and travel also provide situations where property and personal rights of American nationals may be infringed.

What avenues of redress are open to these claimants? The law of international claims is one area where an abundance of substantive law vividly contrasts with a paucity of procedural remedies.[8] As the Committee on International Law of the Association of the Bar of the City of New York has noted:

> The remedies available outside the municipal courts to an individual injured by a foreign State through a violation of international law are limited at best. Should the individual succeed in having his claim espoused by the State of which he is a national (which he ordinarily has no legal right to demand), there is no international tribunal of general and mandatory jurisdiction to which his State may present the claim in the event that diplomatic representations prove ineffectual.[9]

With no international judicial system available, the American claimant and his attorney must look either to the espousal of his

[7] *Ibid.*

[8] Several years ago the Committee on Nationalization of Property of the American Branch of the International Law Association stated that "procedures for the application of the foregoing principles are secondary only to the principles themselves. International Law is characterized by an assertion of rights coupled with an absence of remedies. The consequent fragility of international law needs no elaboration. Any effort to strengthen the rule of law must consider procedure with substance, enforcement with prescription." PROCEEDINGS AND COMMITTEE REPORTS OF THE AMERICAN BRANCH OF THE INTERNATIONAL LAW ASSOCIATION 73 (1957–1958).

[9] COMMITTEE ON INTERNATIONAL LAW OF THE ASSOCIATION OF THE BAR OF THE CITY OF NEW YORK, A RECONSIDERATION OF THE ACT OF STATE DOCTRINE IN UNITED STATES COURTS 1 (1959).

claim by the Department of State or, assuming that the United States has been fortunate enough to negotiate a settlement with the foreign country involved, to the adjudication of his rights by a special *ad hoc* international claims commission or the Foreign Claims Settlement Commission, a municipal agency established in 1954, by the merger of the War Claims Commission and the International Claims Commission, to distribute lump sum settlements to eligible claimants.

The general practitioner, faced with the task of preparing and presenting an international claim to the Department of State or an appropriate commission, is frequently unfamiliar with the problems in this area of the law. A late expert in the field, who served with the Department of State, once complained:

> There is a great lack of knowledge, even on the part of well-trained lawyers, about governmental procedures in the field of protection of Americans abroad and the prosecution of international claims, both as regards settlement out of court and hearings before international tribunals. There is an impression that it is only necessary to inform the Department of State of the claim. But if the American client wants results within a reasonable time, his local attorney must take the initiative and do most of the work.[10]

The onus for ill-prepared claims, though, does not rest solely with the Bar. The traditional memoranda sent by the Department of State to claimants or their attorneys frequently do not answer the complicated procedural problems which have arisen since World War II. The Section of International and Comparative Law of the American Bar Association concluded as far back as

[10] Cowles, *To What Extent Will American Lawyers Need an Understanding of International Law to Serve Clients Adequately During the Last Half of the Twentieth Century?* 7 J. LEGAL ED. 179, 195 (1954).

1944 that the Department of State's legal staff was so limited that "claimants have usually received only perfunctory suggestions with reference to the preparation of evidence." [11] Where, then, can an attorney look for aid in preparing an international claim?

The answer is that no work exists which would be of any aid to him.[12] This book is designed to meet his need. Aside from Chapter I, which is a concise summary of the eligibility of claimants for the benefit of those persons having only a passing familiarity with the law of international claims, the scope of this work is limited to the mechanics of preparing and presenting international claims based upon private grievances,[13] and the discussion will be more descriptive than critical. Furthermore, since the book is primarily aimed at an American audience, the substance of the text will reflect United States law and practice. Whenever possible, current examples will be used and recent decisions cited, making the book an up-to-date source of claims law.

The work should serve diverse purposes in view of the various methods of presenting claims and the correlative necessity of deciding a claimant's exact needs. Great stress will be placed upon the preparation of claims for individual espousal by the Department of State, since this method remains the traditional pro-

---

[11] PROCEEDINGS OF THE SECTION OF INTERNATIONAL AND COMPARATIVE LAW OF THE AMERICAN BAR ASSOCIATION 96 (1944).

[12] The only book concerning the procedural side of international claims published in the United States was THORPE, PREPARATION OF INTERNATIONAL CLAIMS (1924). It dealt primarily with World War I claims against Germany and is completely outdated today. A more recent work, WORMSER, COLLECTION OF INTERNATIONAL WAR DAMAGE CLAIMS (1944), incidentally considered some procedural problems relating to possible claims arising from World War II.

[13] Interstate claims, such as the claim of the United States against the Soviet Union for shooting down an RB-47 over international waters, are not considered, since responsibility for their preparation and presentation rests exclusively with the executive branch of the United States government and is of little concern to the private practitioner.

cedure for presenting international claims. Equal attention will be given to preparing claims for presentation to the Foreign Claims Settlement Commission, a semi-permanent United States agency which in all probability will distribute large claims settlements made in the foreseeable future. Some attention also will be devoted to claims procedure before mixed claims commissions such as the United States–Japanese Property Commission [14] and the United States–Italian Conciliation Commission.[15] These international bodies often have been used to adjudicate great batches of claims between states and may be used again should there be a thaw in the international climate.

While this work is written mainly for claims attorneys and general practitioners who may one day find themselves representing clients with what they believe to be international claims, it is hoped that it also will be of substantial value to government lawyers, whether with the Department of State, the Foreign Claims Settlement Commission, or other federal departments and agencies. Businessmen with foreign interests, who are anxious to calculate the risks of doing business abroad or to evaluate the status of risks already taken, may well make incidental use of the volume. Finally, students of international law concerned with procedural problems of establishing a world rule of law may be interested in examining the experience gained by the United States from nearly two centuries of handling international claims. While this experience has not always been highly satisfactory, it is nevertheless a beginning of an international law of procedure which any future reforms must take into account.

[14] Established under Article II of the Agreement With Japan, June 12, 1952 [1952] 3 U.S.T. & O.I.A. 4054, T.I.A.S. No. 2550.

[15] Established under Article 83 of the Treaty of Peace With Italy, Feb. 10, 1947, 61 Stat. 1410, T.I.A.S. No. 1648.

CHAPTER I

Eligible Claimants

THE traditional rule that only states have rights under international law precludes aggrieved individuals from presenting international claims directly to foreign states.[16] Instead, under the theory that whoever wrongs an individual indirectly injures his state,[17] a claimant must seek redress by demonstrating to his government that it should adopt his private grievance and espouse it as an international claim against the offending foreign state.[18]

The most important task of an American claimant, therefore, is to convince the Department of State (or the Foreign Claims Settlement Commission) that he is an eligible claimant entitled to protection. As Hackworth states:

[16] RESTATEMENT, FOREIGN RELATIONS, EXPLANATORY NOTES § 175, comment *a* at 624 (Proposed Official Draft, 1962).

[17] FCSC, TENTH SEMIANN. REP. 155, 160 (1959) (hereinafter cited "FCSC 1959 REP.").

[18] RESTATEMENT, FOREIGN RELATIONS, Explanatory Notes § 217, comment *a* at 727 (Proposed Official Draft, 1962).

7

The first essential of an international claim is a showing that the claimant is entitled to the protection of the state whose assistance is invoked. . . . Until the right of the claimant to the protection of the state whose assistance is invoked has been established, there is no occasion to consider the facts and law of the case for the purpose of determining whether there is a just grievance against a foreign state.[19]

The purpose of this chapter is to indicate the principal classes of claimants to which the United States extends protection. If a potential claimant does not meet the eligibility tests, he need read no further.

INDIVIDUALS

The most important condition precedent to securing government espousal of an individual's grievance is the requirement that it have been owned by a United States national at the time of loss or injury.[20] The Foreign Claims Settlement Commission, like the Department of State,[21] has consistently taken this position.

It is a well-known and long-established rule, followed without exception by this Commission and its predecessors, that a claim cognizable under principles of international law does not

---

[19] 5 HACKWORTH, A DIGEST OF INTERNATIONAL LAW 802 (1943) (hereinafter cited "HACKWORTH").

[20] See, generally, LILLICH, INTERNATIONAL CLAIMS: THEIR ADJUDICATION BY NATIONAL COMMISSIONS 76–84 (1962) (hereinafter cited "LILLICH"). The term "national" includes both United States citizens and persons owing permanent allegiance to the United States. *E.g.*, 69 Stat. 570 (1955), 22 U.S.C. § 1641(2) (1958). Claims of nonnationals have been allowed in a few exceptional cases. See 5 HACKWORTH 802; LILLICH 76, n. 278.

[21] 5 HACKWORTH 802.

come into existence unless the property which is the subject of the claim was owned by a national of the United States at the time of damage. Otherwise it cannot be said that the United States has received an injury or has a legal cause to complain against another nation.[22]

If the claimant was an American national when his claim arose, which is a matter of municipal law which must be established in each case,[23] it makes no difference whether his nationality was acquired by birth, naturalization, marriage, or otherwise.[24]

In addition to showing American nationality at the time of the claim's origin, the claimant must demonstrate that it has been continuously owned thereafter by American nationals, for "the Government of the United States, as a rule, declines to support claims that have not belonged to claimants . . . from the date the claim arose to the date of its settlement." [25] This continuity of nationality rule has been construed by the Foreign Claims Settlement Commission to require American nationality to the date of the settlement agreement [26] or the date of the filing of

[22] FCSC 1959 REP. 154–55.
[23] See Chapter II.
[24] LILLICH 82. See text note 20 *supra.*
[25] 5 HACKWORTH 804.
[26] The Yugoslav Claims Agreement was so interpreted. FCSC, SETTLEMENT OF CLAIMS BY THE FOREIGN CLAIMS SETTLEMENT COMMISSION OF THE UNITED STATES AND ITS PREDECESSORS 55–58 (1955) (hereinafter cited "FCSC 1955 REP."). It was not necessary for the Commission to decide whether continuous American nationality was required after the date of the agreement. *Id.* at 22, note 1. Compare Clay, *Aspects of Settling Claims under the Yugoslav Claims Agreement of 1948,* 43 GEO. L. J. 582, 596 (1955). Annex A of the 1960 Polish Agreement specifically requires continuous nationality only "to the date of entry into force of this Agreement. . . ." Agreement With Poland, July 16, 1960 [1960] 11 U.S.T. & O.I.A. 1956, T.I.A.S. No. 4545. See Re, *Foreign Claims Settlement Commission of the United States,* in N.Y.S.B.A., REP. OF COMM. ON INT'L L. 19, 21 (1961).

the claim,[27] depending upon whether awards are being made from a lump sum settlement or from vested assets. A claimant's loss of nationality after the applicable date, or his subsequent transfer of the claim to a nonnational, may defeat the claim.

At the other end of the continuity of nationality rule, recent decisions of the Foreign Claims Settlement Commission, based upon international agreements and implementing legislation, have worked peculiar variations. In construing section 303(3) of the International Claims Settlement Act, which provided for the payment of certain contractual and other claims against Bulgaria, Hungary, and Rumania from vested assets,[28] the Commission took the view that the claimant was required to show that he was a national well before the time of loss.[29] This position has been criticized severely as an unwise and unsound departure from the usual international law rule.[30] Conversely, in handling war loss claims arising under section 303(1) of the same act, the Commission in effect held that the claimant need not have been an American national when the loss occurred if he later acquired such nationality by a specific date.[31] In so holding, the Commission pointed out that "the customary rule of international law may be regarded as having been modified by the treaty and by the International Claims Settlement Act." [32] In both of the above instances, the Commission's decisions were limited to claims arising under one ambiguous statute, and they may be regarded as unique opinions having little effect on the traditional rule. Nevertheless, they should serve as red flags to potential claimants, re-

[27] See, *e.g.*, FCSC 1959 REP. 17, 119, 134, 177.

[28] 69 Stat. 572 (1955), 22 U.S.C. § 1641b(3) (1958).

[29] FCSC 1959 REP. 13, 37.

[30] *Id.* at 39–40. See also *Hearing on S. 706 Before a Subcommittee of the Senate Committee on Foreign Relations*, 86th Cong., 1st Sess. 31–32 (1959) (memorandum of Dr. Martin Domke).

[31] FCSC 1959 REP. 104–05.

[32] *Id.* at 102.

minding them to check the Commission's legal standards for each claims program rather than rely automatically on customary international law.

One aspect of the continuity of nationality rule, the problem of the eligibility of naturalized citizens who acquired such status after the date of the loss or injury, has plagued both the Department of State and the Foreign Claims Settlement Commission. The latter, noting that "it has been the position of the Department of State that naturalization is not retroactive so as to justify the espousal of claims arising prior to the acquisition of United States citizenship," [33] has refused to make awards to naturalized citizens who acquired their American nationality after the international wrong took place.[34] Repeated attempts to have Congress modify the rule to permit such awards have failed,[35] with one exception so unusual as not to deserve mention here.[36]

Analogous to the situation of a naturalized citizen is the claim of a national who acquired title to his claim from an alien. Although the various methods of acquiring claims are discussed elsewhere in this chapter,[37] it should be mentioned here that the Department of State [38] and the Foreign Claims Settlement Com-

[33] *Ibid.* ". . . [C]laims of foreigners who, *after* the claims accrued, became Americans . . . can not be espoused by the United States." 5 HACKWORTH 804.

[34] FCSC 1955 REP. 40.

[35] See *Hearing on S. 706 Before a Subcommittee of the Senate Committee on Foreign Relations,* 86th Cong., 1st Sess. (1959).

[36] When surplus monies were left in the Italian claims fund after all claimants who were nationals at the time of their losses had been paid, the Department of State supported special legislation permitting the Foreign Claims Settlement Commission to make awards from this surplus to claimants who became American citizens after their claims arose. LILLICH 79–81. See also Peselj, *The Rule of the Nationality of Claimant, Due Process of Law and the United States Congress,* 53 AM. J. INT'L L. 144 (1959). The chances of such a situation happening again are remote.

[37] See text at note 89 *infra* and following.

[38] 5 HACKWORTH 804.

mission [39] will not accept claims of United States nationals based upon transfers from aliens when the claim arose prior to the date of transfer, since in such a case the claim was not owned by a national at the time of the international wrong.[40] Conversely, when an American claimant loses his nationality after the claim accrues, the continuity of nationality rule will preclude its espousal.[41]

Even when the continuous nationality requirement has been met, problems have arisen when the American claimant was also a national of the foreign country.[42] The traditional international law rule has been that "where the person injured is a dual national, the state of the one nationality is not entitled to espouse the claim against the state of the other nationality." [43] The Department of State, while expressing its disapproval, has acknowledged the "well settled" character of this rule.[44] Thus, although the Department will not refuse to espouse the claim of a dual national when his dominant nationality is American, the chances of its securing compensation for the claimant cannot be assured.[45]

[39] FCSC 1955 REP. 50.

[40] Id. at 165.

[41] 5 HACKWORTH 804. Loss of nationality is a question of municipal law beyond the scope of this work, but it should be noted that many claims are denied on this ground. See, e.g., FCSC 1955 REP. 138–40 and FCSC 1959 REP. 57–58, 69, 138–39, 145 (expatriation); FCSC 1955 REP. 141 and FCSC 1959 REP. 52–53 (voting in foreign election); and FCSC 1955 REP. 141–42 (serving in foreign army and taking oath of allegiance to foreign state).

[42] See, generally, Orfield, The Legal Effects of Dual Nationality, 17 GEO. WASH. L. REV. 427 (1949).

[43] SIMPSON & FOX, INTERNATIONAL ARBITRATION 106 (1959). See RESTATEMENT, FOREIGN RELATIONS, Explanatory Notes § 178, comment a at 633–34 (Proposed Official Draft, 1962).

[44] 5 HACKWORTH 822.

[45] Id. at 819–22. Rode has argued, on the basis of the Merge decision by the United States–Italian Conciliation Commission, that the traditional rule denying claims of dual nationals may "gradually fall into

United States national commissions in the past have both allowed [46] and denied [47] claims by dual nationals. The Foreign Claims Settlement Commission has not considered dual nationality a reason for denying awards.[48]

Closely akin to the dual nationality problem is the difficulty sometimes occasioned by the so-called Calvo Clause.[49] This provision, often found in constitutions of Latin American countries or in contracts they enter into with aliens, purports to preclude an alien's right to seek the diplomatic protection of his government.[50] Under the doctrine, advanced by the Argentine jurist Carlos Calvo, "aliens are not entitled to rights and privileges not accorded to nationals, and . . . therefore they may seek redress

---

disuse. The practical result in this country might be that in the future the Government of the United States will afford protection to its citizens and espouse their personal injury or property damage claims against foreign governments, notwithstanding the fact that the claimants also appear to be citizens of the respondent country." Rode, *Dual Nationals and the Doctrine of Dominant Nationality*, 53 AM. J. INT'L L. 139, 143 (1959).

[46] Crandall, *Principles of International Law Applied by the Spanish Treaty Claims Commission*, 4 AM. J. INT'L L. 806, 814 (1910).

[47] NIELSEN, AMERICAN-TURKISH CLAIMS SETTLEMENT, OPINIONS AND REPORT 12–15 (1937).

[48] In LILLICH 83 it was stated that the Commission "has made awards . . . to persons who were dual nationals." The decisions of the Commission cited as authority actually denied the claims involved, but upon a ground other than dual nationality. In dictum the Commission observed that "we did not deny this claim on the ground that claimant is a citizen of Yugoslavia. . . . For the purpose of emphasis, we add that even if we found affirmatively that a particular claimant had not lost Yugoslav citizenship under the laws of that country, such a finding would not reflect upon his loyalty or attachment to the United States." FCSC 1955 REP. 43, 213–14. The logical implication is that claims by dual nationals will be considered. See note 45 *supra*. See also Rubin, *Nationalization and Compensation: A Comparative Approach*, 17 U. CHI. L. REV. 458, 466, n. 24a (1951).

[49] See, generally, SHEA, THE CALVO CLAUSE (1955).

[50] 5 HACKWORTH 635.

for grievances only before the local authorities." [51] The Department of State has never considered itself bound by the clause,[52] and national commissions have never given it any credence.[53] While the clause therefore will not bar the espousal of a claim or the making of an award, it may trouble a claimant if a Latin American country invokes it in an effort to avoid settling the claim.[54]

PARTNERSHIPS

Partnership claims occur less frequently today than they did in years past, due in large part to the decline of this method of doing business abroad.[55] An American partnership is an eligible claimant when its members are American nationals.[56] If one of the partners is a nonnational, then the remaining American partners will be protected individually to the extent of their interest

[51] *Ibid.*

[52] *Id.* at 637–38. "However, in its conduct of claims practice, the Department of State has, in effect, [given] limited substantive effect to the Calvo Clause." RESTATEMENT, FOREIGN RELATIONS, Explanatory Notes § 207, Reporters' Note at 708 (Proposed Official Draft, 1962).

[53] *Hearing on S. 2528 Before a Subcommittee of the Senate Committee on Foreign Relations,* 77th Cong., 2d Sess. 54 (1942) (remarks of Mr. Lester H. Woolsey). See also AMERICAN-MEXICAN CLAIMS COMMISSION, REPORT TO THE SECRETARY OF STATE 73, 298 (1948).

[54] "As regards state practice, it is difficult to determine the extent to which foreign offices have not espoused claims because Calvo Clauses were involved. But there is some evidence . . . that, where a Calvo Clause is involved, espousal has been infrequent, except where outrageous or manifestly unfair conduct on the part of the respondent state has been involved." RESTATEMENT, FOREIGN RELATIONS, Explanatory Notes § 207, Reporters' Note at 707–08 (Proposed Official Draft, 1962).

[55] See, generally, LILLICH 84–86.

[56] AMERICAN-MEXICAN CLAIMS COMMISSION, REPORT TO THE SECRETARY OF STATE 237 (1948).

in the partnership.[57] Even when the firm is located in a foreign country, the Department of State will espouse a claim based upon the proportionate interest of the firm's American members.[58] Thus, with an occasional exception,[59] both partners and partnerships are eligible claimants if they meet the nationality requirements.

CORPORATIONS

Corporate claims were rare before the century's turn. The Spanish Treaty Claims Commission was the first United States national commission to hold that claims by corporations were compensable.[60] Awards were made to American corporations regardless of the citizenship of their stockholders, even in cases where almost all the stock was owned by nonnationals.[61] The Department of State, while supporting the claim of an American corporation "regardless of the extent of the alien interest in the company," [62] refused to espouse the claims of corporations wholly owned by foreign interests.[63] Thus, as explained by the

[57] *Id.* at 288.
[58] 5 HACKWORTH 828–30.
[59] LILLICH 85.
[60] SPECIAL REPORT OF WILLIAM E. FULLER 29 (1907).
[61] Crandall, *supra* note 46, at 814–15.
[62] 5 HACKWORTH 833.
[63] "[I]t has been the long standing practice of the Department of State to refrain from pressing diplomatically the claims of American corporations in which there was no substantial American interest. The Department does not consider it proper for the Government of the United States to seek to protect, under the cloak of American corporations, interests which are wholly alien. Unless American citizens would derive benefit from the recovery of indemnity in favor of American corporations, the Department does not consider that it would be warranted in pressing a claim diplomatically in behalf of a corporation." *Id.* at 839.

Foreign Claims Settlement Commission, a two-pronged test was applied to determine when a corporation was an eligible claimant:

> The criteria which the Department of State utilized in determining whether to espouse corporate claims consist of two elements.
>
> First, it has required that the corporation be incorporated under laws of the United States or a constituent state. . . .
>
> Secondly, the Department has required that there be a beneficial American interest in such corporation to authorize diplomatic espousal of a claim.[64]

Lump sum settlements [65] and domestic claims legislation [66] since World War II have followed this approach, generally specifying that the latter half of the test is met when fifty per cent or more of the corporation's outstanding capital stock or other beneficial interest is owned by United States nationals.[67]

For a corporation to be an eligible claimant, then, it must have been organized in the United States or a constituent state or other political entity.[68] Moreover, at all times pertinent to the claim it

[64] FCSC 1955 Rep. 41.

[65] Agreement With Rumania, March 30, 1960 [1960] 11 U.S.T. & O.I.A. 317, T.I.A.S. No. 4451; Agreement With Poland, July 16, 1960 [1960] 11 U.S.T. & O.I.A. 1953, T.I.A.S. No. 4545.

[66] 69 Stat. 570 (1955), 22 U.S.C. § 1641(2) (1958); 72 Stat. 527 (1958), 22 U.S.C. § 1642 (1) (1958).

[67] See, generally, Lillich 86–90. The Yugoslav Claims Agreement required only a showing of twenty per cent American interest. Agreement With Yugoslavia, July 19, 1948, 62 Stat. 2658, T.I.A.S. No. 1803. See FCSC 1955 Rep. 41. On the wisdom of utilizing a fixed percentage rather than the flexible standard of substantial American interest, see Clay, *Recent Developments in the Protection of American Shareholders' Interests in Foreign Corporations*, 45 Geo. L. J. 1, 11 (1956) and Rubin, *supra* note 48, at 468.

[68] FCSC 1955 Rep. 76. Thus a foreign corporation, even if 100 per cent United States owned, would not be an eligible claimant. *Id.* at 223.

must have been substantially (generally fifty per cent or more) owned by nationals of the United States.[69] Even when a corporation's stock is nominally owned by United States nationals, the United States would not be "obliged to espouse a claim on behalf of a corporation organized in the United States, if the evidence showed that the real parties in interest were aliens." [70] The Foreign Claims Settlement Commission will "pierce the veil" and deny a claim if the stock, while legally owned by United States nationals, is in fact beneficially owned by aliens.[71]

STOCKHOLDERS

When an individual or a corporate stockholder is a United States national holding stock in either a foreign corporation or an ineligible American corporation,[72] he may be able to secure protection of his proportionate interest in the "nonnational" corporation.[73] According to the Department of State:

The American stockholders in such a case, however, would be able to bring stockholders' claims. *Id.* at 223–24. See text at notes 72–88 *infra*.

[69] FCSC 1959 REP. 131. If this requirement is not met, the United States stockholders may have compensable stockholders' claims. See text at notes 72–88 *infra*.

[70] AMERICAN-MEXICAN CLAIMS COMMISSION, REPORT TO THE SECRETARY OF STATE 195 (1948).

[71] FCSC 1955 REP. 40–42.

[72] If the stockholder's corporation is an eligible claimant itself, the stockholder of course is precluded from bringing a claim. See, *e.g.*, 69 Stat. 573 (1955), 22 U.S.C. § 1641j(a) (1958). The term "nonnational" corporation, to be used below, includes both foreign corporations and ineligible American corporations. Since stockholders may have compensable claims based upon their interests in American corporations which do not meet the eligibility requirements for corporate claimants, *i.e.*, failure to meet the fifty per cent standard, it is a more accurate term than the traditional one of "foreign" corporation. LILLICH 91, n. 351.

[73] 5 HACKWORTH 840–45. See, generally, Clay, note 67 *supra*, and Grav-

Losses sustained by organizations not incorporated in the United States may be the subject of claims by this Government on behalf of American nationals only to the extent of the American ownership of such organizations. For example, if forty percent of the stock of a foreign corporation is owned by American nationals a claim may be filed on behalf of such nationals for forty percent of the losses sustained by the corporation.[74]

The Department will intervene diplomatically, however, only "where there is a substantial American interest in a foreign corporation. . . ." [75] United States national commissions prior to World War II adhered to this view, rendering awards to American stockholders of nonnational corporations in which citizens of the United States had a "substantial and bona fide interest." [76]

While the above test, purposely vague, is still used by the Department of State, it has been replaced in claims programs since the war with a variety of standards governing the eligibility of stockholder claimants. Thus the Yugoslav Claims Agreement of 1948 rejected the "substantial and bona fide interest" test and permitted claims of American stockholders for their proportionate interest in nonnational corporations regardless of the extent of the total American interest therein.[77] With one exception,

---

ing, note 190 *infra*. See also Jones, *Claims on Behalf of Nationals Who Are Shareholders in Foreign Companies*, 26 BRIT. YB. INT'L L. 225 (1949).

[74] 5 HACKWORTH 845.

[75] FCSC 1955 REP. 224. See RESTATEMENT, FOREIGN RELATIONS, Explanatory Notes § 180, comment *b* at 636 (Proposed Official Draft, 1962).

[76] LILLICH 90-91.

[77] Agreement With Yugoslavia, July 19, 1948, 62 Stat. 2658, T.I.A.S. No. 1803. "[C]laims by stockholders were specifically recognized in article 2(c) which provided for claims 'indirectly owned' by United States nationals 'through interests direct, or indirect' in a foreign juridical person or persons." FCSC 1955 REP. 224. Note that the Commission inaccurately limits stockholder claims to claims in "foreign" corporations. See text note 72 *supra*.

this approach was followed in the 1960 Polish Claims Agreement.[78] Under both agreements a stockholder owning only a few shares in a nonnational corporation would be an eligible claimant.[79] Furthermore, the stockholder's ownership interest in the injured or nationalized corporation could be a direct [80] or indirect [81] one.

Another arbitrary standard, in effect a legislative codification of the "substantial and bona fide interest" test,[82] was adopted by Congress in 1955 when it enacted a program providing for the payment of claims against Bulgaria, Hungary, Rumania, Italy, and the Soviet Union. Under this program American stockholders in nonnational corporations had eligible claims only if twenty-five per cent of the corporation's stock was owned by natural persons who were nationals of the United States.[83] If more than seventy-five per cent of the total ownership interest was alien-held, the stockholder was remediless.[84]

In 1958 Congress carved a retroactive exception from the

[78] See Annex A of the Agreement With Poland, July 16, 1960 [1960] 11 U.S.T. & O.I.A. 1956, T.I.A.S. No. 4545. Subdivision g of Annex A requires American interests "substantial in amount" as a condition to the allowance of one particular type of indirect stockholder claim.

[79] Clay, *supra* note 67, at 15. See note 78 *supra* for a possible exception to this statement.

[80] For example, by owning stock in the corporation.

[81] For example, by owning stock in a corporation which, in turn, owned stock in the injured or nationalized corporation. Rubin, *supra* note 48, at 466. See, *e.g.*, FCSC 1955 REP. 173: "[T]he Commission has concluded that it is established that, at the time of the taking of the Apatini property, the latter company was wholly owed by Kispesti; that at that time the claimant was the owner of only 7,560 shares of Kispesti stock, of which a total of 30,000 shares were outstanding; that, accordingly, the claimant was then the owner of an indirect interest, to the extent of 25.2 percent, in the Apatini assets; and that an award should be made to him on that basis."

[82] S. REP. No. 1050, 84th Cong., 1st Sess. 7 (1955).

[83] 69 Stat. 573 (1955), 22 U.S.C. § 1641j(b) (1958).

[84] FCSC 1959 REP. 66, 94.

twenty-five per cent standard [85] by "providing that in claims based upon direct interests in nationalized concerns the 25% requirement shall no longer apply. The amendment did not affect claims based upon indirect interests in nationalized concerns." [86] This double standard also is contained in the Czechoslovakian Claims Act of 1958 [87] and, of necessity, in the Rumanian Claims Agreement of 1960.[88]

The futility of attempting to generalize about stockholder claims is evident from the above discussion. While the Department of State still professes adherence to the "substantial and bona fide interest" test, the Foreign Claims Settlement Commission, its hands tied by variable standards found in executive agreements and municipal legislation, must adjudicate stockholder claims on a purely *ad hoc* basis. Although the general trend is toward the allowance of direct stockholder claims regardless of the extent of the American interest in the nonnational corporation, the claimant when seeking compensation from the Commission should first consult the specific legal standards of the particular claims program to determine his eligibility.

[85] 72 Stat. 531 (1958), 22 U.S.C. § 1641j(b) (1958).

[86] FCSC 1959 REP. 212. For claims where this modified standard was applied, see *Id.* at 93, 120, 218. Indirect stockholder claims often involve extremely complicated fact situations. See, *e.g.*, *Id.* at 64–66.

[87] 72 Stat. 529 (1958), 22 U.S.C. § 1642e(b)(c) (1958).

[88] Article II of the Agreement With Rumania, March 30, 1960 [1960] 11 U.S.T. & O.I.A. 318, T.I.A.S. No. 4451. This inartistically drawn provision, drafted to conform to the earlier statutory provisions under which the Rumanian claims were adjudicated (see note 83 *supra*), contains several discrepancies, one of which is considered in LILLICH 93, n. 361 and Christenson, *The United States–Rumanian Claims Settlement Agreement of March 30, 1960,* 55 AM. J. INT'L L. 617, 624, n. 41 (1961).

OTHER CLAIMANTS

Often a claim, having accrued to an eligible claimant, passes to another party before settlement. Here two problems arise. The first, briefly considered above, is whether the continuous nationality requirement has been met.[89] The second is whether the party seeking the award has the standing, under municipal and international law, to bring the claim as successor to the original claimant. The situations in which these problems most frequently occur will be considered below.

1. *Administrators.* Claims by administrators representing deceased claimants have been allowed by the Department of State [90] and the Foreign Claims Settlement Commission.[91] In a typical case, where a United States national had died owning a claim against a foreign country and his estate was in the process of being wound up, "the Commission recognized the duly qualified administratrix of such estate as the proper party claimant and made an award in favor of such person as administratrix of the decedent's estate. . . ." [92] Should a claimant die after filing a claim, his administrator may request substitution as party claimant; if the administrator fails to act, the Commission will issue its decision in the name of his estate.[93]

While the nationality of the administrator is presumably im-

---

[89] See, especially, text at notes 37–41 *supra.*

[90] 5 HACKWORTH 849–51. See also Article 10(B)(2) of the Rules of Procedure of the United States–Japanese Property Commission, Appendix F.

[91] FCSC 1955 REP. 222; FCSC 1959 REP. 163, 220.

[92] FCSC 1955 REP. 222.

[93] 45 C.F.R. § 531.5(j)(1)(3) (1960). *Cf.* FCSC 1955 REP. 20 (award made to claimant's estate when executor failed to submit proof of his capacity).

material,[94] the continuous United States nationality of the decedent must be shown.[95] If the decedent dies after the claim is filed, the Commission may make its decision without inquiring as to the nationality of the heirs.[96] Indeed, it has actually rendered awards with knowledge that one of a decedent's heirs was an alien.[97] Whether the Department of State would go so far is a matter of speculation.[98]

2. *Assignees.* Claims by assignees will be espoused by the Department of State and allowed by the Foreign Claims Settlement Commission only if the assignor, as well as the assignee, is a United States national.[99] Obviously, the assignment of a claim by a United States national to an alien defeats the claim.[100] Conversely, claims based upon assignments by aliens to United States nationals are denied.[101] As a practical matter, after the deadline for filing claims the Commission will not permit the amendment of a claim to reflect its assignment,[102] except where the assignment comes into being by operation of law.[103]

3. *Executors.* Claims by executors will be treated by the Department of State [104] and the Foreign Claims Settlement Commission [105] just like claims by administrators.

4. *Guardians.* In a claim where a minor child was entitled to compensation under the terms of a lump sum settlement, the

[94] LILLICH 98.
[95] FCSC 1959 REP. 69.
[96] FCSC 1955 REP. 21–22. *But see* Item No. 1 of the instructions for completing Form No. 709, Appendix B, and note 26 *supra*.
[97] FCSC 1955 REP. 21–22.
[98] *Cf.* 5 HACKWORTH 849–51.
[99] *Id.* at 846–48; FCSC 1955 REP. 221. See also FCSC 1959 REP. 203, 221.
[100] LILLICH 94–95.
[101] FCSC 1955 REP. 50, 165; FCSC 1959 REP. 258.
[102] 45 C.F.R. § 531.5(K) (1960).
[103] FCSC 1959 REP. 199.
[104] See note 90 *supra*.
[105] FCSC 1955 REP. 20; FCSC FOURTEENTH SEMIANN. REP. 158, 176 (1961) (claims denied on other grounds). See also note 96 *supra*.

Foreign Claims Settlement Commission recognized the guardian of the minor's estate as the proper party claimant and made an award accordingly.[106] The Department of State presumably would take the same position.

5. *Heirs*. Until recently claims presented by heirs were denied.[107] The Foreign Claims Settlement Commission, however, has allowed claims by heirs based upon their inheritance of both real [108] and personal [109] property. Widows [110] and children [111] are the most common claimants. Since the law of the situs determines the descent of real property [112] and the succession laws of the decedent's domicile the descent of personal property,[113] extensive investigations of foreign and domestic inheritance laws are often required.

The heir's claim may be one which directly accrued to the decedent and then passed to the heir [114] or, as is more common in recent claims programs, it may be one which occurred after the heir allegedly inherited the property.[115] Except in the latter situation, where the heir acquired his right to the decedent's property

---

[106] FCSC 1955 Rep. 222.

[107] Lillich 96–97.

[108] FCSC 1955 Rep. 126–33.

[109] *Id.* at 59–60.

[110] *Id.* at 224; FCSC 1959 Rep. 222.

[111] FCSC 1955 Rep. 59–60; FCSC 1959 Rep. 219–20.

[112] See note 108 *supra. But see* note 114 *infra.*

[113] FCSC 1955 Rep. 59. Personal property includes accrued claims. See note 114 *infra.*

[114] *Id.* at 222. In such cases the heir's eligibility is determined by the succession laws of the decedent's domicile, even when the claim is based upon the taking of real property. Compare text at notes 112–13 *supra.* "In those claims where the recorded owner of the property died intestate subsequent to . . . the date of taking, the Commission held that the deceased died seised of a chose-in-action and that such property right passed to the heirs of the decedent in accordance with the laws of intestacy of the decedent's domicile and accordingly considered such heirs as the proper party claimants. . . ." *Ibid.*

[115] *Id.* at 132–33, 145–46.

before the claim's accrual, the continuity of nationality rule bars an award to an heir when the decedent was an alien, the theory being that an American heir cannot inherit a right, *i.e.*, an espousable claim, that his alien ancestor did not possess.[116] Thus where an alien is involved the heir must show that he became entitled to the ownership of the property prior to its taking.[117]

Recorded Department of State practice with respect to claims by heirs is scanty.[118] While the Department undoubtedly prefers that claims be brought by executors or administrators, it will give appropriate consideration to claims by heirs when the latter are unable to obtain judicial determination of their successor interests.

6. *Legatees.* While heirs as well as administrators have been deemed proper parties claimant in case of intestacy, legatees have had to defer to executors when testate succession was involved.[119] Regulations of the Foreign Claims Settlement Commission omit reference to them,[120] and in the case of one claim, where the executor died subsequent to the filing of the claim, the Commission rendered an award to the claimant's estate, rather than to his legatee, "in order to preserve the rights and interests of those who may eventually be entitled to collect such award." [121]

7. *Receivers.* A duly appointed receiver of an American corporation which has ceased doing business is a proper party claimant and is entitled to an award in such capacity.[122] Similarly, a

---

[116] See text at notes 37–40 *supra*.

[117] *Id.* at 132–33.

[118] *Cf.* 5 HACKWORTH 850.

[119] See text at notes 104–05 *supra*.

[120] 45 C.F.R. § 531.5(j)(3) (1960).

[121] FCSC 1955 REP. 20.

[122] *Id.* at 46. *Cf. Id.* at 224 (reference to continued United States nationality of all of the corporation's stockholders in claim by receiver presumably not a condition to the latter's eligibility). See also Annex B of the Agreement With Poland, July 16, 1960 [1960] 11 U.S.T. & O.I.A. 1957, T.I.A.S. No. 4545.

trustee in bankruptcy or an assignee under an assignment for the benefit of creditors would be an eligible claimant.[123]

8. *Subrogees*. Under municipal law, when an insurer indemnifies its insured under a policy of insurance it is subrogated to the rights of the insured. Applying this principle to the international claims field, the Foreign Claims Settlement Commission has rendered awards in favor of American insurers, based upon the amounts they have paid to injured American insureds.[124] To render such subrogee claims compensable, it must be shown "that the carriers as well as the insureds were nationals of the United States at the time of loss," [125] and that the claims were "continuously owned thereafter by a United States national or nationals." [126]

9. *Miscellaneous Claimants*. Claims by creditors, mortgagees, pledgees and similar persons have been handled by the Department of State and the Commission. Whether such claimants may present claims is a question of substantive international law which, while generally beyond the scope of this work, will be considered briefly in Chapter IV. They are not considered in this section, which is limited to the status of parties claiming as successors to presumably eligible original claimants.

[123] LILLICH 95.

[124] FCSC 1959 REP. 150–51. *Cf. Id.* at 24–25 (United States subrogated to individual's claim to the extent the latter had been compensated by private law).

[125] *Id.* at 151. See also LILLICH 96.

[126] FCSC 1959 REP. 152.

The Preparation of an
International Claim: Nationality

PRELIMINARY CONSIDERATIONS

THE preparation of an international claim actually begins when the claimant considers whether he meets the eligibility requirements summarized in Chapter I. If he satisfies these requirements, and if his claim is a valid one under customary international law or the legal standards of the particular claims program,[127] then the accumulated evidence supporting the claim must be marshaled and organized to document a formal claim.

---

[127] As stated in the Preface, this work does not purport to cover, except incidentally, the substantive law of international claims. An entire volume would be needed to deal adequately with the subject, which has not been treated systematically for years. Among the dated works of most help to a claimant, see BORCHARD, THE DIPLOMATIC PROTECTION OF CITIZENS ABROAD (1916) and EAGLETON, THE RESPONSIBILITY OF STATES IN INTERNATIONAL LAW (1928). See also 5 HACKWORTH 471–851 and the three volumes of WHITEMAN, DAMAGES IN INTERNATIONAL LAW (1937–1943) (hereinafter cited "WHITEMAN").

Similar in nature to the civil law "dossier," the documented claim takes the place of what, in the ordinary law suit, would be the trial. While certain formalities must be adhered to, the properly presented claim is a creature of common sense, and any reasonable and credible proof should be considered for possible inclusion.

The first step in preparing a formal claim is to draw up a statement of claim. Claimants and their attorneys should realize the importance of preparing, in affidavit form, a detailed narrative of the facts upon which the claim is based. This affidavit should be entitled simply "Statement of Claim" and should contain a clear presentation of each element of the claim together with the relevant supporting facts.[128] Additional proof, particularly if in documentary form, should be placed in annexes or exhibits accompanying the statement of claim. These annexes and exhibits should be clearly identified in the body of the statement of claim after the allegations they are meant to support.

There will be variations in the exact form which a statement of claim takes, depending upon whether the claim is being submitted to the Department of State for possible espousal to a foreign country or to a national or international commission which has jurisdiction over the claim. The Foreign Claims Settlement Commission, for instance, has its own forms which should be used as the basis for preparing a claim to be presented to it.[129] International claims commissions also have special procedures under which claims are prepared for presentation by United States government agents.[130] Since different persons will examine

[128] A sample statement of claim in affidavit form may be found in Appendix A.

[129] A sample claims form of the Foreign Claims Settlement Commission may be found in Appendix B. See also 45 C.F.R. §§ 500.1–501.7, 531.1–531.4 (1960).

[130] For example, see Appendix F for Articles 10–14 of the Rules of Procedure of the United States–Japanese Property Commission, adopted

the claim no matter what agency it comes before, it is important to prepare a lucid and accurate statement of claim, backed up by whatever supporting evidence is available, that will preclude controversy among the examiners concerning its relative merit. If a claim is demonstrably valid to most eyes, the chances of obtaining an award with the least possible delay naturally will be increased.

The statement of claim should be prepared in triplicate for the Department of State, with each copy being signed and notarized. The same number of copies of supporting documents should be submitted, also duly authenticated.[131] One copy of the completed claim is retained by the Department for its files and, assuming that the claim is deemed to be meritorious and that political conditions are favorable for espousal, two copies are forwarded by the Department to the American embassy in the foreign country against which the claim is brought. One copy is retained by the embassy and the other copy is submitted to the foreign office of the country concerned. If an American agent is to present claims to an international commission, he may be required to submit additional copies of the claim and supporting documents. After receiving copies of the claim, the American embassy or agent retains one copy and presents the original to the appropriate authority, together with any additional copies which may be required under special rules of procedure.[132] The Foreign Claims Settlement Commission now requires that the statement of claim be filed in triplicate.[133]

Briefs on questions of international law to accompany the

March 31, 1959, under the Agreement With Japan, June 12, 1952 [1952] 3 U.S.T. & O.I.A. 4054, T.I.A.S. No. 2550.

[131] Any supplemental statements of claim should be in the same form and clearly marked as such.

[132] See note 130 *supra* (Article 10).

[133] See the general statement of the instructions for completing Form No. 709, Appendix B.

statement of claim, if thoroughly researched and carefully written, can be very persuasive. The American agents before both the United States–Italian Conciliation Commission and the United States–Japanese Property Commission have utilized briefs prepared by claimants' attorneys, and the use of briefs before the Foreign Claims Settlement Commission is a common occurrence.

As a general rule, the statement of claim to be presented to the Department of State must contain the essential facts relating to the following elements: (1) that the claimant is eligible to make the claim; (2) that the claimant or his predecessor in interest sustained an international wrong; (3) that as a result of the wrong the claimant or his predecessor in interest was damaged in a certain amount; and (4) that the claimant without success has exhausted all administrative and judicial remedies in the foreign country, or that no remedies exist or that if remedies exist it would be futile to resort to them. Normally the claims forms used by the Foreign Claims Settlement Commission require similar information, although each form varies according to the program involved and none so far has required information or proof as to the exhaustion of local remedies.[134]

Statements of claimants, according to the Department of State, "even when under oath, must be corroborated by other evidence." [135] In a special memorandum regarding claims against Cuba, the Department announced that it would not "be in a position to take up a claim or make representations to the Cuban Government . . . without proof, preferably, documentary evidence which it could submit or bring to the attention of the Cuban Government," adding that "unsupported general statements about such matters would not as a rule have sufficient evidentiary value to warrant action." [136]

[134] *Ibid.*
[135] See Appendixes C and D.
[136] Department of State Memorandum entitled "Debts Owed to Amer-

The documents or exhibits in support of a claim to be filed with the Foreign Claims Settlement Commission should, if possible, be originals.[137] Copies of public documents are acceptable if certified by their custodian.[138] Similarly, the best evidence available should accompany a statement of claim presented to the Department of State. Best evidence may include original documents, duly authenticated certified copies thereof, certified copies of public documents and *ex parte* affidavits.[139]

In preparing affidavits, claimants and other affiants should avoid exaggerated and false statements, since penalties for the use of false statements include: (1) the institution of criminal proceedings against the person perjuring himself; [140] (2) the refusal or withdrawal of Department of State support in settling the claim; or (3) the denial of the claim by the Foreign Claims Settlement Commission.[141]

Each affidavit used as evidence should contain the full name, age, place of birth, place of residence, nationality, and present occupation of the affiant. The affidavit also should state his address and occupation at the time the events he describes occurred and specify whether he has any personal interest in the claim. This information adds credibility to and increases the probative value of the testimony contained in the affidavit. While a claimant preparing a claim for submission to the Department of State must reduce all testimony to affidavit form, the Foreign Claims Settlement Commission has the power to assist claimants by issuing subpoenas, taking testimony under oath, making its own in-

---

ican Nationals by Private Parties and Concerns in Cuba," March 1, 1961, reprinted in 56 AM. J. INT'L L. 166 (1962). *But see* FCSC 1959 REP. 68, 121 (awards rendered despite lack of corroboration).

[137] See note 133 *supra*.
[138] 45 C.F.R. § 531.3 (1960).
[139] SANDIFER, EVIDENCE BEFORE INTERNATIONAL TRIBUNALS 165 (1939).
[140] 18 U.S.C. § 1001 (1958).
[141] See note 133 *supra*.

vestigations, and authorizing depositions and written interrogatories.[142]

Before either the Commission or the Department, all supporting documents in a foreign language must be accompanied by a verified translation into English. The translation should be certified by the translator under oath, stating that he is thoroughly familiar with the foreign language and that to the best of his knowledge his translation is true and accurate.[143] Documentary evidence filed with the Department of State or most commissions becomes part of the permanent records of the United States government or of the commission. In cases of necessity, however, the claimant may make arrangements, within the discretion of the agency involved, for the return of any needed documents.

With the above preliminary considerations in mind, the first problem of proof facing the claimant is establishing his United States nationality. Claimants must be prepared to prove that: (1) the person or persons sustaining the alleged international wrong were nationals of the United States on the date of the wrong; and that (2) the person or persons and any successors in interest to the claim had American nationality continuously thereafter, at least until the presentation or filing of the claim.[144] The means of establishing nationality, as will be seen below, differ according to whether the claimant is a natural person, a partnership, or a corporation.

INDIVIDUALS

Natural persons satisfy the United States nationality requirement by demonstrating that they are citizens of the United States

[142] 45 C.F.R. §§ 501.1, 501.5 (1960).
[143] 45 C.F.R. § 531.3(b) (1960). See also note 133 *supra*.
[144] See text at notes 20–27 *supra*.

and were such on the date of the wrong. Their citizenship may be acquired at birth, by naturalization, by marriage or through their parents. Only in rare instances are persons who are not United States citizens entitled to be considered United States nationals.[145]

A certified copy of a birth certificate will establish that an individual was born a United States citizen. When the birth occurred in United States territory (*jus soli*), the certificate itself, properly certified by the custodian of the records, will suffice. When birth took place upon foreign territory to American parents, citizenship is acquired through the properly preserved citizenship of one or both parents (*jus sanguinis*). Therefore a person born abroad to American parents should furnish, in addition to his own birth certificate, the birth certificates of the parent or parents through which he obtained citizenship. If the parent or parents obtained citizenship by naturalization, the evidence regarding such naturalization must be obtained through the Immigration and Naturalization Service, as explained below.

Establishing nationality by birth raises no problems in those cases where birth certificates are available. However, if a certificate does not exist or cannot be obtained, proof of American birth is more difficult. First of all, general United States practice requires a satisfactory explanation why a certificate is unavailable. This explanation may take the form of an affidavit of the efforts made by the claimant or his representative to obtain a certificate. It should be supported by evidence such as letters between the claimant and custodians of records at the place of birth or at church archives. Secondly, when a birth certificate is unavailable a claimant has the burden of proving citizenship at birth by sufficient other evidence, and this task necessarily becomes increasingly difficult the older the claimant grows. The kinds of persua-

---

[145] For example, see 66 Stat. 238 (1952), 8 U.S.C. § 1408 (1958). See also note 20 *supra*.

sive evidence on this point include certificates of baptism signed soon after birth,[146] certified copies of the baptismal records,[147] passports,[148] affidavits of at least two persons having personal knowledge of the date and place of birth,[149] certified copies of written entries in official journals and family Bibles or other records (providing that proof is offered pertaining to their authenticity and age). When the claim is being presented to an international claims commission, consular certificates to the effect that a person is registered as an American national with the American consulate are prima facie evidence of nationality.

A useful statutory procedure exists for establishing the United States citizenship of claimants who have derived their citizenship through the naturalization of a parent, or the naturalization or citizenship of a husband, or who are citizens of the United States by birth abroad to American parents. They may apply to the Attorney General of the United States for a certificate of citizenship, which will be furnished if proper proof is presented and if the claimant is at the time within the United States.[150] Another possible method for establishing citizenship is to bring an action for a judgment declaring that the claimant is a United States national.[151] Such action must be based upon a denial, on the ground that the person is not a United States national, of some right or privilege of nationality.[152] Persons frequently use this procedure to obtain a judicial determination of nationality after a denial of a passport by the Department of State based upon lack

[146] See Appendix E.
[147] See Item No. 9 of the instructions for completing Form No. 709, Appendix B.
[148] *Ibid.*
[149] See Appendix E.
[150] 66 Stat. 263 (1952), 8 U.S.C. § 1452 (1958).
[151] 28 U.S.C. § 2201 (1958). See, *e.g.,* Tijerina v. Brownell, 141 F. Supp. 266 (S.D. Texas, 1956).
[152] 66 Stat. 273 (1952), 8 U.S.C. § 1503 (1958).

of nationality.[153] It is conceivable that a person with an international claim, which the Department of State or the Foreign Claims Settlement Commission refused to recognize for alleged want of nationality, could seek a judicial determination of the question of nationality, alleging a denial of a privilege of American nationality. Although such an action could not compel the Department of State to present a claim through diplomatic channels or require the Commission to render an award, it might clear up a doubtful nationality question that had previously precluded its acceptance.

If a claimant or any predecessor in interest is a citizen by naturalization or marriage or through his parents, he should establish his American nationality by requesting the Immigration and Naturalization Service, Department of Justice, Washington 25, D.C., to furnish evidence of his nationality to the Department of State.[154] Claimants before the Foreign Claims Settlement Commission must complete in duplicate a special DSP-13 form entitled "Request for Confirmation of Naturalization," which the Commission will use to obtain the needed information directly.[155] It has been held by an international claims commission that a certificate of naturalization is only prima facie evidence of nationality for purposes of determining whether the commission has jurisdiction over the claim, and it may be rebutted by extrinsic

[153] See, *e.g.*, Luk v. Dulles, 268 F.2d 824 (9th Cir. 1959). The Sixth Circuit has held that this procedure, insofar as it might be available to a claimant denied an award by the Foreign Claims Settlement Commission on the ground that he was not a national, was superseded by the Commission's explicit no-review statute. Zutich v. Gillilland, 254 F.2d 464, 466 (6th Cir. 1958). Although the claimant presumably asked only "for a judgment declaring that he was a national of the United States," the court treated the action as one involving judicial review, holding that the statute "left it without jurisdiction to review the Commission's decision." *Id.* at 465. Compare the text above following this note.

[154] See Appendix E.

[155] See note 147 *supra*.

evidence showing noncompliance with the applicable United States statute.[156] When writing to the Immigration and Naturalization Service, a claimant should give his full name, age, date and place of naturalization, the name of the court before which he appeared, the number of the certificate issued by the court and, if he claims citizenship through spouse or parents, relevant information concerning their citizenship, the date of marriage or birth, and the like.

Since a citizen may lose his American nationality and citizenship by certain voluntary acts,[157] a claimant should set forth in either the statement of claim or a supporting affidavit an explanation for any activity raising the question of possible loss of nationality.[158] If at any time a claimant has lost his United States nationality, a detailed statement should be attached to the statement of claim indicating when and where such nationality was lost, and when and where it was reacquired, together with all pertinent documentary evidence.[159]

Once a claimant has shown that he or his predecessor in interest was an American national on the alleged date of an international wrong, he next must establish that the claim remained continuously in the hands of American nationals until it was settled or filed.[160] The required continuity is best shown by proof

[156] RALSTON, VENEZUELAN ARBITRATIONS OF 1903 38 (1904). See also Flagenheimer (United States v. Italy), OPINIONS, UNITED STATES–ITALIAN CONCILIATION COMM., ESTABLISHED UNDER ARTICLE 83, TREATY OF PEACE WITH ITALY, CONCLUDED FEB. 10, 1947, Decision reprinted in 53 AM. J. INT'L L. 944 (1959).

[157] 66 Stat. 267 (1952), 8 U.S.C. § 1481 (1958), as amended.

[158] See note 41 *supra.*

[159] See Item No. 11 of the instructions for completing Form No. 709, Appendix B.

[160] See text at notes 26–27 *supra.* Since nationality after settlement or filing may not be required, claimants whose health is a matter of concern, and who have heirs who are not American nationals, should file statements of claim as soon as possible to preserve the continuity of nationality to the date of settlement or filing. See text at note 368 *infra.*

of the American nationality of each and every successor in interest, together with affidavits setting forth any facts which would clarify and explain questions regarding any possible break in the chain of American nationality.

Persons who are nationals of the United States but not citizens thereof are sometimes entitled to diplomatic protection. The United States in its discretion may espouse an international claim on behalf of persons such as seamen on American vessels, members of the military or naval forces of the United States when owing allegiance thereto, and persons residing in outlying possessions of the United States who are natives of their locale.[161] A mere declaration of intention to become a United States citizen, filed with the proper authorities and accompanied by permanent residence in the United States, is insufficient to establish American nationality or the right to American protection.[162] Proper documentation of the nationality or right to protection of persons who are not United States citizens includes certificates of birth in a United States territory or possession, affidavits of persons with special knowledge, e.g., masters of vessels in the case of seamen, and certified copies of enlistment forms or oaths.

PARTNERSHIPS

Although partnerships usually are considered legal entities in international law, the nationality of claims submitted on behalf of partnerships is determined by proving the nationality of the individual partners.[163] If one or more partners is not a national of the United States entitled to diplomatic protection, the American partners should present claims on their own behalf as in-

---

[161] See notes 20 & 145 *supra*.
[162] FCSC 1959 REP. 34–35.
[163] See notes 55–57 *supra*. See also 1 Whiteman 133.

dividuals, based upon their proportionate interest in the partnership, as well as in the partnership name. The name and nationality of each partner who is a nonnational should be given in the statement of claim in order to fix the exact interest of the American claimants. Each partner who is a claimant in his own right should establish nationality by means of the same type of evidence used by individual claimants.

Modern claims practice would seem to require the furnishing of a certified copy of the partnership agreement or articles of association which establish the status of the partnership continuously from the date of the international wrong to the submission or filing of the claim in the partnership's name.[164] Such documents should show the principal place of business of the partnership and the countries and states in which it is registered or qualified to do business, as well as the residences and ownership interests of each partner or other beneficial owner.

While traditional international law has not treated partnerships in the same way as it has corporations, being more concerned with the nationality of the partners than the place of organization or doing business,[165] the increased tendency to recognize partnerships as legal entities may justify presenting a partnership claim in its own name when, despite the presence of nonnational interests, the partnership is an American one with a substantial American ownership interest.[166] As stated above, however, each partner in the abundance of precaution should sign the statement of claim and furnish evidence of his own United States nationality. Then, should the partnership's claim be denied, an award

---

[164] See Item No. 1 of the instructions for completing Form No. 709, Appendix B.

[165] RALSTON, THE LAW AND PROCEDURE OF INTERNATIONAL TRIBUNALS 139–41 (1926) (and 1936 supplement at 65–66). See text at note 163 *supra* and note 168 *infra*.

[166] *Cf.* FELLER, THE MEXICAN CLAIMS COMMISSIONS 116 (1935). Compare text at note 56 *supra*.

may still be made to its American partners for their proportionate interest in the enterprise.[167]

CORPORATIONS

Claims on behalf of corporations are submitted in the corporate name. The nationality of the corporation is generally established by producing an authenticated copy of its certificate of incorporation in the United States or a constituent state or other political entity, showing the status of the corporation on the date of its loss and continuously down to the date of presentation or filing of the claim.[168] Because incorporation in the United States does not in itself make the corporation an eligible claimant, documents also should be submitted establishing the citizenship of its principal officers and directors. In addition, an affidavit by the secretary or other principal officer of the corporation should be filed certifying as to the outstanding capital stock or proprietary interest owned by United States nationals at the time of the corporation's loss and continuously thereafter.[169] Claims programs administered by the Foreign Claims Settlement Commission in recent years have required at least fifty per cent beneficial ownership to be in the hands of United States nationals.[170]

Ordinarily, it is a difficult task to determine the nationality of stockholders or beneficial owners of stock, especially if the corporation has outstanding bearer shares. While the place of residence often is stated on the stock registry of the corporation for use in paying dividends, the nationality of the stockholders is

[167] See text at note 57 *supra*.

[168] See text at note 68 *supra*.

[169] See Item No. 12 of the instructions for completing Form No. 709, Appendix B.

[170] See text at notes 64–69 *supra*.

not so indicated. For the small or close corporation the requirement of furnishing the information is not burdensome. For the larger corporate claimant with hundreds of outstanding shares and different stock issues, however, the task is harder. The secretary's affidavit will usually suffice as to the percentage of stock beneficially owned by United States nationals. If in doubt, the secretary should indicate the percentage of stockholders residing in the United States, or in its territories and possessions, and state to the best of his knowledge the percentage of foreign beneficial ownership of stock registered in the name of United States residents and the American beneficial interest in stock held by persons abroad.

If a substantial stockholder of the claimant corporation is itself a corporation, proof of the nationality of the stockholder corporation also is required. It should take the same form as proof of the corporate claimant's nationality.

CHAPTER III

The Preparation of an
International Claim: Ownership

WHILE traditional international law has treated ownership of an international claim as accruing to a state rather
than to the aggrieved individual, the theoretical debate over
whether countries or individuals own international claims is
largely ignored when persons present claims either to the Department of State or the Foreign Claims Settlement Commission.
Thus, although a claimant may be a United States national continuously from the date of the claim's accrual, he still is not an
eligible claimant unless he can prove by evidence that the claim
was owned by a United States national from the date it arose.[171]

[171] See text at notes 20–27 *supra*. " 'Another general principle of international law which could come into play in the consideration of these
claims is the general rule that such a claim must have been continuously
owned by a United States national (not necessarily the same one) at all
times between the time the claim arose and the presentation of the claim,
whether directly to the foreign government or before the appropriate
adjudicating body. Thus, if at any time subsequent to the time of the
loss, a claim originally accruing to a United States national had become

The Foreign Claims Settlement Commission has denied many claims on the sole ground that the claimant failed to establish this necessary element of ownership.[172]

When the same person has owned the claim from the date of its accrual to the time of settlement or filing, there is little difficulty in establishing the claimant's eligibility. If, however, a change in the ownership of the rights to present the claim and collect an award has occurred by reason of death, assignment, or some other transfer, the chain of title to these rights must be proved to convince the Department or the Commission that the person presenting the claim is the proper party claimant. This chapter will consider the ways and means of satisfying the requisite ownership requirement.

WRONGFUL DEATH CLAIMS

Under United States practice, an international claim based upon a wrongful death accrues not to the decedent's estate but rather to those persons such as the decedent's wife, children or parents who have sustained a direct, measurable loss from being deprived of his support, association, and care.[173] The only ownership problem with respect to the claim is the identification of a survivor of the decedent and the connection of the survivor with some demonstrable injury. Proving an ownership interest in the claim may be accomplished by affidavit of the survivor himself and by documentary evidence establishing the survivor's relation to the decedent. In the event of several survivors, a joint

---

vested in a nonnational (whether by inheritance, purchase, or otherwise), the claim would not be espoused even if it was thereafter reacquired by a United States national.' " FCSC 1959 REP. 16–17.

[172] *Ibid.* See also *Id.* at 85–86, 113, 193.

[173] I WHITEMAN 83–84, n. 187. See also *Id.* at 706.

claim may be filed with a separate calculation of damages for each survivor.

Since a claimant is not eligible if he has assigned, waived, or otherwise lost his right to make a claim, it is wise when establishing eligibility in the statement of claim to make a full disclosure of facts relating to any possible assignment, waiver, or other act which might suggest relinquishment of the right to the claim. Whenever ownership is asserted by reason of assignment, inheritance, or other transfer of the claim, proper documentation is necessary to prove continuity of title. Each and every successor to the original survivor must then be identified and his right to the claim verified, down to the person finally presenting the claim.[174]

PERSONAL INJURY CLAIMS

From the viewpoint of claims procedure, the main difference between a personal injury and a wrongful death claim is that in the former the individual physically injured is generally the claimant owning the right to bring the claim. Identity of the claimant is accordingly easier to establish than is identity of a survivor-claimant in wrongful death cases. The two types of claims are sometimes brought by the same claimant when, as a result of personal injuries, a person dies leaving survivors. The decedent's personal injury claim would be inherited by his survivors, who in addition would have an independent wrongful death claim.

A claimant can establish his ownership of a claim based upon personal injuries by proving that he was the person who was physically injured or that he has succeeded to the claim of such a person. Affidavits of persons who were eye witnesses to the in-

[174] See text at notes 89–126 *supra* and notes 204–211 *infra*.

cident as well as an affidavit of the injured person constitute proof of identity.[175] Newspaper accounts and police records and reports are helpful in identifying persons involved and witnesses present, and they also constitute useful secondary evidence. Cooperation of the police and other authorities in the foreign country can be facilitated by using the American embassy or the nearest American consulate to obtain necessary introductions or appointments.

Property Claims

Proving ownership of claims for loss of or damage to property entails something more than simply identifying the original claimant and establishing continuity in the title to the claim. When property is involved, there are two elements to ownership. The first is the interest in property which has been damaged by the wrongful act or omission attributable to a foreign country. The second is the interest in the resulting claim for compensation which is derived from the injury to the interest in property owned by the claimant or his predecessors in interest.

The initial ownership of a claim for a wrong to property, being derivative, is established by proving ownership of the property lost or damaged. Since the claim is the right to be compensated for the injury to the property, the claimant must link his ownership of this right to the original injured party. If two or more persons have interests in the property, the resulting claims are in the same proportion as the interests in the property.

It is possible that a claim is all that remains of an interest in property. For example, if all private real property is taken over

[175] See Appendix C. It is frequently possible to include such statements in affidavits used to prove other elements of a claim, such as damage or the wrongful act.

by a foreign country under nationalization laws, a former owner is entitled to claim compensation for the property taken. The claim is assignable and inheritable.[176] However, the claim may be only for damage to the property, such as may result from temporary requisitioning of the property for governmental purposes. In this case both the ownership of the property itself and the ownership of the claim for damages are transferable and inheritable separately, according to local law.[177] Under United States practice, a claim for damage to property is not transferred with the property damaged unless so expressed in a contract of sale.[178] The main reason for this rule is that market value at the time of sale usually determines the selling price. If the former owner has repaired at his own expense or the property has been reduced in value, the seller would bear the loss and thus should retain the claim.[179] When some consideration for the damage claimed is given or is expressed in an agreement, the claim may then pass with the property.

The ownership of real property is established according to the law of the country where the wrong occurred.[180] In civil-law countries, the local land registers or land records are themselves

---

[176] See text at and accompanying notes 107–118 *supra*.

[177] *Ibid.*

[178] Paragraph 16(5) of a mimeographed Department of State Memorandum Regarding Claims of American Nationals Under Provisions of the Treaty of Peace With Japan, dated June 20, 1952, provided: "If the claimant is a successor in interest to damaged property of an Allied national for which compensation is requested, evidence should be furnished establishing the fact that the claimant is also the successor to the claim for compensation." See Items No. 1 & 14 of the instructions for completing Form No. 709, Appendix B.

[179] Carnelli (United States v. Italy), OPINIONS, UNITED STATES–ITALIAN CONCILIATION COMM., ESTABLISHED UNDER ARTICLE 83, TREATY OF PEACE WITH ITALY, CONCLUDED FEB. 10, 1947, Decision No. 5 (mimeographed, 1952).

[180] FCSC 1959 REP. 185.

evidence of ownership.[181] Since in common-law countries recordation is only constructive notice of title, a deed or other muniment of title usually is required.[182] The Department of State prefers certified copies of deeds, extracts from land registers or contracts of purchase.[183] In the absence of such documents, construction contracts, receipt books, bonds for warranty deeds, receipts for taxes, and letters and records of grantors have substantial probative value.[184]

For personal property, affidavits regarding possession and title at the time of loss or damage will suffice to establish ownership, although any documentary evidence available is preferable. Valid evidence includes documents such as sales receipts, invoices, bills of lading, and other commercial papers. In proving an ownership interest in shares of stock of nationalized corporations, claimants at times have been assisted by the Foreign Claims Settlement Commission's liberal approach. The Commission has given credit to uncorroborated testimony regarding the claimant's ownership interest, although in such cases it has rendered awards of less than the full amount claimed.[185]

Once it has been established that the claimant or his predecessor in interest owned the property lost or damaged at the time of the alleged wrong, and hence became the owner of the resulting claim, it is necessary to prove continuity in the title to the claim, especially where the claim is presented by a person other

[181] FCSC 1955 REP. 181: "While it is true that title to real property under general rules of the civil law does not pass until the transfer to the title is recorded, such a requirement has been abandoned by the laws and acts of the Government of Yugoslavia which had the purpose of socialization or collectivization of property."

[182] See Appendix D.

[183] See sample statement of claim in affidavit form, Appendix A, for examples.

[184] FCSC 1955 REP. 225.

[185] FCSC 1959 REP. 66–68, 120–21. See text at and accompanying note 283 *infra*.

than the original injured party. Contracts of assignment, wills, court inheritance proceedings, and affidavits may be submitted to satisfy this requirement. Local law regarding ownership transfer should be proved if there is any question of law involved in the chain of title to the claim.[186]

SPECIAL PROBLEMS OF PROVING OWNERSHIP

1. *Corporate Claims.* When United States corporations are claimants, special problems of proof are presented.[187] If the corporation owns real or personal property which is damaged, nationalized, or otherwise taken by the foreign country, the corporate ownership of the resulting claim is proved in the usual manner by establishing ownership in the property itself. However, when the property is owned indirectly through a subsidiary foreign corporation, ownership of the claim is proved by establishing the parent corporation's substantial beneficial interest in its foreign subsidiary as well as the subsidiary's direct ownership of the property concerned.[188] Proving interest in a subsidiary foreign corporation, according to the Foreign Claims Settlement Commission, may be accomplished by filing the following proofs:

> The certificates of stock held by the claimant evidencing its ownership in its subsidiary company, an affidavit from one of the claimant's officers relating to its ownership of such stock, indicating when, where and how acquired and the consideration paid, certified copies of balance sheets or other records of the claimant evidencing such ownership as of the date of tak-

[186] FCSC 1955 REP. 185, 211. See text at and accompanying notes 107–118 *supra*.

[187] See LILLICH 86–90 and text at notes 60–71 & 168–70 *supra*.

[188] This situation is analogous to the typical stockholder's claim. See notes 190–203 *infra*.

ing and thereafter, and certified copies of its subsidiary's records reflecting such ownership during the same period.[189]

2. *Stockholder Claims.* More difficult problems of proof are raised when the injured company is either a foreign corporation or an ineligible American corporation. While in either case the nonnational corporation is itself precluded from bringing a claim, United States stockholders are usually able to file claims based upon their proportionate interests in the injured concern.[190] Since the corporation is the initially wronged party, all stockholder claims are in effect "indirectly owned" by the claiming stockholders.[191] However, in settlement agreements and claims legislation a distinction is made between "direct" and "indirect" stockholder claims.[192]

Ownership of those claims which are based upon direct stock holdings in nonnational corporations is established by proving title to shares held by the claimants. Actual stock certificates, trust certificates, or receipts for bearer shares held by a nominee (as, for instance, street certificates) are the best means of establishing a direct ownership in a corporation.[193] When the corporation has been nationalized without payment of compensation, proof of ownership of the claim is complete once the above evidence is furnished. But if the corporation has been injured by the taking of or damage to its property,[194] additional proof of the corporate ownership of the property taken or damaged must be provided.[195]

[189] FCSC 1955 REP. 116.
[190] See text at notes 72–88 *supra.* See also LILLICH 90–94. The most recent discussion of stockholder claims is Graving, *Shareholder Claims Against Cuba,* 48 A.B.A.J. 226, 335 (1962).
[191] FCSC 1955 REP. 224.
[192] See text at and accompanying notes 80–81 *supra.*
[193] See text at note 189 *supra.*
[194] See, *e.g.,* 72 Stat. 529 (1958) 22 U.S.C. § 1642e(b) (1958).
[195] See text at notes 188–89 *supra.*

Proving ownership of those claims based upon indirect stock holdings in nonnational corporations is much more complex, since such claims often involve layers of corporations with vastly interrelated structures.[196] Suppose, for example, that a United States stockholder owned stock in an English corporation which, in turn, owned stock in a Czech corporation which had suffered a loss or had been nationalized.[197] What would the American stockholder have to prove in order to establish his indirect claim?

First of all, the claimant must submit proof of his direct ownership of shares in the English corporation.[198] Secondly, the claimant must demonstrate the latter's direct ownership interest in the Czech concern. This requirement is met by producing certified copies of stock certificates held by the English corporation or certified copies of its balance sheets or other records indicating that it owned such stock.[199] Finally, unless the Czech corporation was nationalized, in which case proof of ownership of the indirect claim is complete once the above evidence is furnished, the claimant must prove that the Czech corporation actually owned the property at the time it was taken or damaged. Certified copies of its corporate books, certified copies of land records or deeds, and supporting affidavits of corporate officers will establish this requirement.

While the above evidence constitutes sufficient proof of a stockholder's ownership interest in an indirect claim, it should be recalled that such a claim, unlike a direct stockholder claim, often requires a further showing that at least twenty-five per cent of the outstanding capital stock of the injured or nationalized

[196] FCSC 1959 REP. 64–66, 80–84.

[197] See note 81 *supra*. This situation reflects the typical indirect claim. See Item No. 10 of the instructions for completing Form No. 604, in FCSC, FOURTEENTH SEMIANN. REP. 61–62 (1961).

[198] See text at note 193 *supra*.

[199] See text at note 189 *supra*.

corporation was beneficially owned by nationals of the United States at the time of loss.[200] Thus, in the above example, the United States stockholder would have to show that he, alone or with other Americans, owned twenty-five per cent of the Czech corporation.[201] Proof of the percentage his shares bore to the total capital stock of the English company, plus proof of the percentage the latter's shares in the Czech corporation bore to the total capital stock of that concern, would have to be furnished.[202] Certified copies of corporate books and stock registers, together with affidavits from appropriate corporate officials, are the best methods of showing the required American interest.

Several general observations may be made concerning both types of stockholder claims. In either case it must be established that the nonnational corporations involved have not settled the claim and that it has not been assigned or transferred. Verified affidavits of corporate officials are adequate for this purpose. If the claim has been settled, assigned, or transferred, then evidence must be furnished about any consideration received by the corporation.[203]

3. *Derivative Ownership of Claims.* When a claimant alleges title to a claim by reason of inheritance, assignment, subrogation, or the like, he must show continuous American nationality in his

---

[200] See text at notes 75–88 *supra.*

[201] See note 81 *supra.*

[202] Compare FCSC 1959 REP. 80–84 (claim allowed) with *Id.* at 64–66 (claim denied).

[203] In one case an American stockholder held shares in an English company which, after having had property taken by Yugoslavia, had established a claim before the British Foreign Compensation Commission. The Foreign Claims Settlement Commission, reversing its prior position that the stockholder was barred by the action of the English company in filing its claim, rendered an award in favor of the stockholder for his proportionate share in the value of the property taken by Yugoslavia, less any and all payments made to the English company. FCSC 1955 REP. 61–62.

predecessors in interest and in himself.[204] Furthermore, after satisfying the requirement that the claim originally accrued to his initial predecessor in interest, he must trace by valid evidence the course of title to himself.

A person claiming title by will must place among his exhibits a certified copy of the will plus proof that it has been duly admitted to probate.[205] Any final distribution decrees must be part of the evidence submitted. If a claimant inherited by intestate succession, he should submit a certified copy of the record of judicial distribution of the estate or its provisional administration.[206] A claim on behalf of an estate by its administrator or executor must provide similar evidence.[207] Affidavits should be used to explain missing documentary evidence and to supplement other documentary evidence.[208]

When a claimant has taken title to a claim under an assignment, he should submit a copy of the contract by which he acquired it.[209] If the claimant is an insurance company claiming as subrogee to an injured insured, the contract of insurance and all relevant conditions of performance, including the subrogation clause, must be set out.[210] Other derivative claimants, such as trustees in bankruptcy, should file proper documentary evidence attesting to their status as such.

In the event that two or more derivative claimants are in disagreement as to the title to a claim, the matter is a dispute which must be resolved by court action either before or after an award.

[204] See text at notes 89–126 *supra*.
[205] See Item No. 1 of the instructions for completing Form No. 709, Appendix B.
[206] *Ibid.*
[207] *Ibid.*
[208] See Item No. 14 of the instructions for completing Form No. 709, Appendix B.
[209] FCSC 1959 REP. 258.
[210] *Id.* at 150–51.

As a matter of practice, the Department of State and the Foreign Claims Settlement Commission will render an award to one of the contending claimants, leaving the parties to the courts to correct any possible error in the determination of title.[211]

[211] While municipal courts have jurisdiction to determine title to claims, they do not have jurisdiction to review the decision of the Department or the Commission as to the validity and amount of awards. LILLICH 58–70. See text at notes 351–353 and 406–419 *infra*.

CHAPTER IV

The Preparation of an International Claim: Wrongful Act

PREPARING proof of the wrongful act alleged in the statement of claim lies at the heart of an international claim. In general, the following proof is useful in establishing the wrongful act: affidavits of the claimant, survivors, or eyewitnesses to the act, identifying the responsible persons, officials, or agencies and describing in detail the facts as they were observed; newspaper accounts of the wrong; certified police reports; certified records of court proceedings; statements of American foreign service officers familiar with or investigating the case; properly verified photographs of the relevant physical scene of the incident; and any written statements, decrees, or orders by officials of the foreign government. Unsworn, unverified statements, while they may be considered in proving the wrong, are given less weight. Aid in gathering evidence sometimes may be obtained from the American officer handling protection matters in the country in which the alleged wrong took place.

Particular problems of proof will be discussed below under the following categories: (1) wrongs against persons; (2) wrongs to interests in property; (3) wrongs involving contracts; and (4) wrongs occurring during time of war.

WRONGS AGAINST PERSONS

Claims based upon personal injury or death are proved in much the same manner as ordinary personal injury and wrongful death actions in municipal courts. The main difference concerns the use of oral testimony. The Department of State has no administrative procedures for the examination or cross-examination of witnesses, although under the rules of the Foreign Claims Settlement Commission witnesses may be examined and cross-examined.[212] Thus proof consists primarily of documentary evidence submitted with the statement of claim. Such evidence generally varies from ex parte affidavits of the injured party, or persons with firsthand knowledge of the facts alleged, to police reports by local authorities.[213]

A claimant has the burden of proof and must establish by convincing evidence that the alleged injury or death was caused by the wrong of a foreign country.[214] A wrong is directly attributed to a country by proof that acts of its officers were wrongful under international law and that such acts occurred in the performance of official duties.[215] A country is not responsible for the

[212] 45 C.F.R. § 531.6(c) (1960).

[213] See Appendix C.

[214] 45 C.F.R. § 531.6(d) (1960); FCSC 1955 REP. 97–98; FCSC 1959 REP. 104; FCSC FOURTEENTH SEMIANN. REP. 112–13 (1961).

[215] FCSC 1955 REP. 163. See also RESTATEMENT, FOREIGN RELATIONS § 173 (Proposed Official Draft, 1962).

private wrongs of its citizens to aliens unless there is an accompanying denial of justice, as that term has come to be understood in international law.[216] A denial of justice is established by showing that no adequate remedy was afforded for particular acts or omissions by officials or courts, resulting in a failure to meet the minimum standards of international law.[217]

Proof of wrongful acts by officials of a foreign government may be very difficult unless eyewitnesses are found who are willing to give statements under oath. While police reports sometimes provide valuable information, they are often unduly favorable to the official involved, who frequently is influential with the local police. Newspaper accounts also can be helpful, but generally they are accorded little weight unless the story contains statements of eyewitnesses who can be properly identified and from whom affidavits may be obtained confirming the account.

Obtaining evidence can be a frustrating experience. For example, while proof that a high-ranking foreign official assaulted an American in public might be obtained from personal observers by diligent effort, if the assault occurred in a government office or a jail it would be almost futile to seek corroborative first-hand testimony. Circumstantial evidence, therefore, might be the only possible means of corroborating a wrongful act. In proving that a wrongful act of an official was committed during the perform-

[216] 5 HACKWORTH 471, 526.
[217] "Denial of justice" is an elusive term used in many different contexts. See RESTATEMENT, FOREIGN RELATIONS, Explanatory Notes § 169, comment *c* at 609 (Proposed Official Draft, 1962). Attempts have been made to define it in terms of specific rules. *Id.* at §§ 182–7. See, generally, FREEMAN, THE INTERNATIONAL RESPONSIBILITY OF STATES FOR DENIAL OF JUSTICE (1938). See also Fitzmaurice, *The Meaning of the Term "Denial of Justice,"* 13 BRIT. YB. INT'L L. 93 (1932); Lissitzyn, *The Meaning of the Term Denial of Justice in International Law,* 30 AM. J. INT'L L. 632 (1936); Spiegel, *Origin and Development of Denial of Justice,* 32 AM. J. INT'L L. 63 (1938); Puente, *The Concept of "Denial of Justice" in Latin America,* 43 MICH. L. REV. 383 (1944).

ance of official duties, statements of higher responsible authorities, if they can be obtained, would be the best evidence. Eyewitness accounts, news items, or admissions by the wrongdoer himself could contain inferences that he was acting in an official capacity.

An act of a minor official, employee, or soldier of a foreign government, even though it arises during performance of his official duties, may not be sufficient to obligate the country under international law without some further dereliction by officials with some authority.[218] However, under modern practice regarding the payment of compensation *ex gratia,* there are increasing grounds for asking a country to pay compensation for death or injury to persons resulting from wrongs by its employees and soldiers.[219] Such claims are usually satisfied under special administrative procedures.[220]

Evidence relevant in establishing a denial of justice arising after a wrongful act of a foreign official includes the following: transcripts of grossly unfair trials; reports of decisions of courts or administrative authorities unjustly denying redress for private wrongs; affidavits regarding discriminatory treatment of an American national in his attempt to obtain private redress or in the application of the law of the foreign country to his detriment; and sworn statements regarding the refusal of the executive authority of the foreign country to carry out a court order favorable to an injured United States national.

[218] 5 HACKWORTH 563. Compare RESTATEMENT, FOREIGN RELATIONS § 173, Reporters' Note at 621 (Proposed Official Draft, 1962).

[219] 5 HACKWORTH 580–81.

[220] See NATO Status of Forces Agreement, June 19, 1951, art. VIII, paras. 5–7 [1953] 4 U.S.T. & O.I.A. 1792, T.I.A.S. No. 2846. See also the United States procedures under the so-called "Foreign Claims Act" designed "to promote and maintain friendly relations through the prompt settlement of meritorious claims" arising from acts or omissions of United States military forces abroad. 10 U.S.C. § 2734 (1958).

Circumstantial evidence again may be the only available means of proving a denial of justice. For example, if a claim is based upon a failure of a foreign government to apprehend and punish a private offender, direct evidence would be hard to obtain. But if it is common knowledge, established by statements of local residents, that a person accused of injuring or killing an American in violation of the local criminal law was in the vicinity, and that fact was communicated to the police without any response or investigation, then an unfavorable inference could be drawn against the foreign country.[221] Even more troublesome to obtain is proof that a mob was not kept under control or that its members were not punished subsequently for any crimes.[222]

WRONGS TO INTERESTS IN PROPERTY

If a foreign country fails to pay just compensation for property of an American national damaged or taken by it, a duty arises under international law to make appropriate reparation to the United States on behalf of its injured national.[223] A claim based upon property loss may result from the total destruction of the property or from its taking, nationalization, expropriation, or confiscation, whether by law or illegally, so long as the wrongful taking can be attributed to the foreign country. Property damage may result from wrongful acts resulting in partial

---

[221] The classic case is the claim of Janes (United States v. Mexico), [1926–1927] OPINIONS OF COMM'RS UNDER THE CONVENTION CONCLUDED SEPT. 8, 1923, BETWEEN THE UNITED STATES AND MEXICO 108 (1927). There an affidavit of a witness indicated the dilatory conduct of Mexican police in failing to apprehend a murderer when a Mexican official was given immediate notice of the crime.

[222] 5 HACKWORTH 662–65.

[223] RESTATEMENT, FOREIGN RELATIONS § 190 (Proposed Official Draft, 1962).

destruction, such as willful or wanton damage to cultural or art objects, or failure to keep requisitioned property in good repair.

If the foreign country takes property under a general nationalization or confiscation law, which on its face does not measure up to the standards imposed by international law, there is little difficulty in proving the international wrong. Examples include the nationalization, confiscation, and other taking of property after World War II by the Eastern European countries [224] and, more recently, by the Cuban expropriation and confiscation laws and decrees.[225] In such cases the general law itself usually need not be proved, since the Department of State and the Foreign Claims Settlement Commission will take notice of it. However, since "a claim for the nationalization or other taking of property does not arise until the possession of the owner is interfered with," [226] a specific application of the general law to the claimant's property must generally be established [227] by submitting orders, judicial decisions, decisions of local "peoples' committees" or official written notices to the claimant.

One problem of considerable importance here is the date on which the taking occurred. It becomes crucial when the claimant is a naturalized citizen and the question is raised whether he was an American national on the date of the taking. If the claimant acquired United States citizenship after the general law was

[224] See Doman, *Postwar Nationalization of Foreign Property in Europe,* 48 COLUM. L. REV. 1125 (1948); Gutteridge, *Expropriation and Nationalisation in Hungary, Bulgaria and Roumania,* 1 INT'L & COMP. L. Q. 14 (1952); Ujlaki, *Compensation for the Nationalization of American-Owned Property in Bulgaria, Hungary and Rumania,* 1 N.Y.L.F. 265 (1955). For a very useful book considering, among other problems, these takings of property, see WHITE, NATIONALISATION OF FOREIGN PROPERTY (1961).

[225] These laws and decrees were held to violate international law in Banco Nacional de Cuba v. Sabbatino, 193 F. Supp. 375 (S.D.N.Y. 1961).

[226] FCSC 1955 REP. 213.

[227] *Id.* at 154. *But see* note 229 *infra.*

passed he may not be an eligible claimant.[228] The intent of the general law itself usually governs the date title passes.[229] The Foreign Claims Settlement Commission determined that a nationalization decree issued subsequent to the Yugoslav Nationalization Law of April 28, 1948, was merely procedural, title having effectively passed on the date of the general law.[230] However, the reasonableness of time within which a foreign country specifically applies its general law may be relevant. It is questionable, for instance, whether a person would lose his right to protection simply because he was not a national on the date of the enactment of an old law used many years later by a foreign government in an attempt to evade international responsibility by imposing what in effect would be a retroactive taking.[231]

If a claim is based upon a taking under a general law not amounting to a nationalization program, such as eminent domain procedures, a translation of the specific law or decree under which the property was taken should be included with the evidence, in addition to certified copies of any official judicial or administrative action in which adequate compensation was denied. If property is taken illegally by ultra vires government action,[232] affidavits of persons having knowledge of the wrongful

[228] See text at and accompanying notes 33–36 *supra*.

[229] With respect to the Hungarian nationalization decrees the Commission held that "in the absence of compelling evidence to the contrary, it will adhere to the principle that the effective date of taking is the date of publication of the nationalization decree." FCSC 1959 REP. 86.

[230] FCSC 1955 REP. 154.

[231] Thus, if the Yugoslav Government took American property in 1958 under its general Nationalization Law of 1948, when all claims under the 1948 Agreement With Yugoslavia had long since been settled, would the taking be effective from the date of the general law and, therefore, be discharged, or would the United States have a right to demand additional compensation?

[232] "Where property has actually been taken by the Government of Yugoslavia under claim of ownership, it would constitute a 'taking' within

act are required. These affidavits should specify the nature and dates of the acts and identify all persons involved, especially government officials. Preliminary correspondence with the Department of State or the Foreign Claims Settlement Commission often will indicate whether the general law must be proved in addition to the particular law or decree. When a decree has not been issued, translated land records, properly certified by their custodian, are invaluable evidence of a taking if the transfer of title to the government has been recorded.

A problem frequently arises when primary evidence, such as special decrees, court orders, or land records are not obtainable because the foreign government is unwilling to issue copies of its official documents for the claimant's use against it. In such a case secondary evidence is the only method of proof. Usually something more than the statement of the claimant himself is required.[233] Sworn statements from relatives, friends, or acquaintances living in the foreign country are particularly helpful if they indicate personal knowledge of an eviction or official acts inferring transfer of ownership or use of property to the foreign government.[234] Since the use of secondary evidence to establish claims may in effect penalize persons whose claims have been established by primary evidence, by diluting the amount available to all claimants from a limited fund, its use is not favored by the Foreign Claims Settlement Commission.

Although in some foreign countries title to real property does not pass until the transfer of the title is recorded, "constructive"

---

the meaning of the Yugoslav Claims Agreement, even if this had been accomplished without legal proceedings of any kind or even with a statutory basis for it in Yugoslav law." FCSC REP. 160. See also *Id.* at 163.

[233] *But see* note 185 *supra* and note 283 *infra*.

[234] FCSC TWELFTH SEMIANN. REP. 4 (1960) (sources in Germany and Austria drawn upon for information assisting in the proof of claims against Czechoslovakia).

or "effective" takings by foreign governments under programs of "creeping nationalization" have been considered international wrongs even when legal title had not passed to the foreign country.[235] Proof of such a wrong is sometimes difficult, particularly when the title to the property nominally remains in the claimant. The following evidence is most helpful: statements by occupants of the property, statements of account for rents controlled by the foreign government, statements regarding the period of time that an owner is deprived of possession, and regulations of the foreign country restricting or denying rights of ownership. Evidence of constructive or effective takings also may be acquired through an attempt by the owner to regain possession of his property. The refusal of possession, coupled with the denial of compensation, is usually in the form of an official statement or action by an administrative or judicial authority. Whatever denial is communicated to the claimant, even if it is only a letter from the appropriate officials, would be probative of a wrong by the foreign country.

Intervention in the management and control of a business, farm, or other property may constitute a constructive or effective taking, depending upon the facts surrounding the intervention.[236] If it is pursuant to an economic reform program, which appears to transfer the means of production to the state, general proclamations or other evidence of such purpose would add weight to the contention that the intervention was a taking, although title remained undisturbed. A physical inspection of the business, farm, or other property might also indicate whether the taking

[235] FCSC Thirteenth Semiann. Rep. 23–24 (1960); FCSC 1959 Rep. 61; FCSC 1955 Rep. 181. See also Restatement, Foreign Relations § 197 (Proposed Official Draft, 1962). Claims for "creeping nationalization" are recognized expressly by Articles I(A) and II(b) of the Agreement With Poland, July 16, 1960 [1960] 11 U.S.T. & O.I.A. 1953–1954, T.I.A.S. No. 4545. See Rode, *supra* note 3, at 455.

[236] FCSC 1959 Rep. 53–54, 131–32.

was temporary or permanent.[237] Other corroborative evidence might include requisition orders for personal property, receipts, inventory lists, affidavits of witnesses or officials, and pertinent correspondence.

No difficulty in proving an outright taking of property arises when extracts of land records in a foreign country can be obtained or when documents of official action regarding the property of an American national are mailed to him. However, a serious problem of proof occurs when records and documents cannot be obtained through ordinary means. Should a question regarding the date of taking also be present, the need for primary evidence increases. A combination of effort, both private and governmental, often will bear fruit. Much evidence regarding property taken in Czechoslovakia after World War II, for example, was obtained for claimants by the Foreign Claims Settlement Commission through contacts in Germany and Austria.[238] The Commission also established an office in Warsaw to assist claimants in procuring evidence for use in establishing claims under the 1960 Agreement with Poland.[239] Moreover, Commission rules permit the use of interrogatories and cross-interrogatories to obtain testimony from abroad.[240]

Wrongs to property or interests in property not amounting to a taking may occur when a foreign government takes possession of or interferes with property, real or personal, and does not pay for such use or interference. Wrongs also may occur when property is damaged, destroyed, or lost through acts or omissions attributable to a foreign country. Modes of interference such as

[237] The Foreign Claims Settlement Commission made such inspections in connection with the Polish claims program. FCSC FOURTEENTH SEMIANN. REP. 18 (1961).

[238] See note 234 *supra*.

[239] FCSC FOURTEENTH SEMIANN. REP. 18 (1961).

[240] 45 C.F.R. § 501.5(b)(g) (1960).

trespass, use, occupation, sequestration, requisition, destruction, damage, or detention are established either by submitting the order or decree issued by the foreign authorities or by submitting affidavits of witnesses with personal knowledge of the facts constituting the wrongful acts. In addition, evidence connecting such acts to the foreign government, such as identification of the responsible official directing soldiers or police to occupy or take possession of private property, should be furnished.

WRONGS INVOLVING CONTRACTS OR CONCESSIONS

It has been stated frequently that the United States will not protect its nationals when they have been injured by a foreign country's breach of contract in the absence of a showing of a denial of justice.[241] A distinction has been drawn between an ordinary breach of contract and one where the breach is effected by the arbitrary use of a governmental power, with international responsibility arising only in the latter instance.[242] International liability also may occur when a foreign country takes the contract right of an American claimant,[243] since a contract right is a property interest.[244] Just what contract rights are interests in property falling within the international rules relating to the taking of property is not altogether clear.[245]

[241] 5 HACKWORTH 611; FCSC 1959 REP. 189.

[242] AMERICAN-MEXICAN CLAIMS COMMISSION, REPORT TO THE SECRETARY OF STATE 540 (1948).

[243] FCSC FOURTEENTH SEMIANN. REP. 119 (1961).

[244] RESTATEMENT, FOREIGN RELATIONS, Explanatory Notes § 200, comment *a* at 692 (Proposed Official Draft, 1962). What constitutes the taking of contract rights presents other problems. See FCSC 1955 REP. 156–59 and note 245 *infra*.

[245] The Foreign Claims Settlement Commission has wrestled with the problem and, in view of varying agreements, statutes, and other factors, has arrived at different conclusions for different claims programs. For

Proof of a wrongful breach of a contract with a foreign country includes: (1) establishing the contractual obligation on the part of the foreign government and the corresponding right in an American national by means of certified copies of the contract or concession agreement; (2) proving the breach of the contract by documents such as legislative enactments or other official acts denying, abrogating, or repudiating contract rights or refusing to perform when a legal duty to do so is clear; (3)

---

example, *bondholder* claims were allowed against Bulgaria, Hungary, Rumania, and the Soviet Union (FCSC 1959 REP. 13, 29, 89, 180–207 *passim*) but were denied as to Italy, Yugoslavia, and Poland (FCSC 1959 REP. 142–43; FCSC 1955 REP. 36–39; FCSC FOURTEENTH SEMIANN. REP. 196–97 [1961]). Against Czechoslovakia one type of bonds was deemed compensable and another not. FCSC FOURTEENTH SEMIANN. REP. 8, 115–16, 119–20. Claims for the loss of *bank deposits* were permitted against Czechoslovakia, the Soviet Union, and Yugoslavia where it could be shown that the deposit was actually taken by an act of nationalization. FCSC FOURTEENTH SEMIANN. REP. 7–8, 116–17, 124–26 (1961); FCSC 1959 REP. 209–11, 223–24, 246–73 *passim;* FCSC 1955 REP. 22. See also FCSC 1959 REP. 17–20 (similar claims against Bulgaria, Hungary, and Rumania not compensable in the absence of a showing that the deposits were nationalized or otherwise taken). *Unsecured creditors'* claims based upon debts owed by nationalized concerns were not allowed against Czechoslovakia, Hungary, Rumania, and Yugoslavia (FCSC FOURTEENTH SEMIANN. REP. 120–22 [1961]; FCSC 1959 REP. 72–79, 117–19; FCSC 1955 REP. 66–67, 83, 84–86), at least where such debts had not, in fact, been confiscated by special decree, law, or administrative decision of the foreign country. *E.g.,* FCSC FOURTEENTH SEMIANN. REP. 11 (1961). Debts claims against nationalized concerns, however, are specifically provided for in Article II(c) of the Agreement With Poland, July 16, 1960 [1960] 11 U.S.T. & O.I.A. 1954, T.I.A.S. No. 4545. *Secured creditors'* claims, for instance those of mortgagees and pledgees, generally have been held compensable. FCSC FOURTEENTH SEMIANN. REP. 11, 122–23 (mortgagee); FCSC 1959 REP. 225–26 (pledgee); FCSC 1955 REP. 58–59, 92 (pledgee and mortgagee). As is obvious from the above, no clear-cut rules can be laid down. The claimant or his attorney must refer to the legal standards governing the specific claims program. It is reasonable to say, though, that the trend is toward the allowance of these claims based upon some sort of "taking."

establishing the failure to obtain a remedy in the administrative or judicial process of the foreign country by furnishing records of the proceedings before an appropriate agency or court or by proving that no remedy is available; and (4) showing that the breach was not justified by any act on the part of the claimant, which necessitates submitting proof of compliance with the claimant's duty to perform his part of the contract.

As stated above, contracts with American nationals which have been breached rather than taken by a foreign government traditionally have not been espoused by the Department of State unless the breach was accompanied by a denial of justice.[246] The term denial of justice in this context means either that no remedy has been afforded for the breach by the courts or agencies of the foreign country, or that the remedy provided fails to meet the minimum standards of international law.[247] The lack of a remedy is established by furnishing copies of decrees denying access to courts or agencies, or by submitting certified copies of laws passed depriving the claimant of remedies for the breach of a contract. Proving that a decision of the highest court or administrative tribunal of the foreign country does not meet the minimum standards of international law is more difficult, especially when an American claimant received treatment equal to that which nationals of the foreign country would have received. The principal problem here is to show the arbitrariness of the proceedings, the complete unreasonableness of the decision, or the capricious nature of the result.

Regarding the breach of contracts between American nationals and private parties in the foreign country, a 1961 Department of State memorandum on private debts owed to Americans by Cubans states the general rule:

[246] See note 241 *supra*.
[247] RESTATEMENT, FOREIGN RELATIONS §§ 184–6, 198 (Proposed Official Draft, 1962).

A legal basis for an international claim against the Cuban Government . . . would not arise unless an American national attempted to collect a debt by exhausting the legal remedies provided by Cuban law and sustained a denial of justice, as that term is understood in international law, such as denial or unwarranted obstruction of access to Cuban courts, gross deficiency or delay in judicial processes, manifestly unjust judgment or an atmosphere of hostility or prejudice which would make it futile to attempt to exhaust legal remedies.[248]

It seems apparent that, should a lump sum settlement ever be negotiated with Cuba, procedures would be provided for settling private debt claims.[249]

When a contract between an American national and a foreign country or one of its nationals is "taken" by the foreign government,[250] the taking usually is established by submitting copies of the contract or concession agreement,[251] together with copies of any law, decree or order by which the claimant's contract rights were canceled or taken. In addition, it should be shown that no remedy has been afforded and that just compensation has not been paid.[252]

[248] Department of State Memorandum entitled "Debts Owed to American Nationals by Private Parties and Concerns in Cuba," March 1, 1961, reprinted in 56 AM. J. INT'L L. 166 (1962).

[249] As they were after World War II with respect to Germany. Agreement on German External Debts, Feb. 27, 1953 [1953] 4 U.S.T. & O.I.A. 443, T.I.A.S. No. 2792.

[250] See text at notes 243–45 *supra*.

[251] *Cf.* FCSC 1955 REP. 22 (photocopy of passbook to prove bank deposit).

[252] RESTATEMENT, FOREIGN RELATIONS § 198 (Proposed Official Draft, 1962).

Wrongs Occurring During Time of War

Historically there has been a theoretical distinction between war loss based upon the ordinary conduct of hostilities, for which no international responsibility is incurred except as otherwise provided by a treaty of peace, and claims for damage based upon the violation of the rules of war or neutrality.[253] Contemporary practice, however, provides for both types of claims in treaties of peace and domestic claims legislation.[254] Whichever legal base is used, war claims are established in much the same way as are claims for wrongs to persons or property. With the old distinction between war loss and war damage largely ignored, the question of damage is of greater significance than the element of wrong. Thus, if it is established that damage was caused by the

[253] FCSC 1955 Rep. 349. See also WCC Report, H.R. Doc. No. 67, 83d Cong., 1st Sess. 113–15 (1953).

[254] Language in the treaties of peace after World War II with Italy, Bulgaria, Hungary and Rumania indicated an intention to compensate all loss caused by the war. "In cases where property cannot be returned or where, as a result of the war, a United Nations national has suffered a loss by reason of injury or damage to property in Italy, he shall receive from the Italian Government compensation in lire to the extent of two-thirds of the sum necessary, at the date of payment, to purchase similar property or to make good the loss suffered." Treaty of Peace With Italy, Feb. 10, 1947, art. 78, para. 4(a), 61 Stat. 1404, T.I.A.S. No. 1648. Language in the other treaties of peace was similar. The Foreign Claims Settlement Commission, pursuant to domestic legislation, adjudicated claims arising under the treaties of peace with Bulgaria, Hungary and Rumania. 69 Stat. 571–72 (1955), 22 U.S.C. § 1641b(1) (1958). See FCSC 1959 Rep. 2. The Commission also adjudicated claims against Italy under the so-called Lombardo Agreement With Italy, Aug. 14, 1947, 61 Stat. 3962, T.I.A.S. No. 1757. See 69 Stat. 572 (1955), 22 U.S.C. § 1641c (1958). See also FCSC 1959 Rep. 2–3. Other such claims were referred to the United States–Italian Conciliation Commission established under Article 83 of the Treaty of Peace with Italy. See text at note 15 *supra*.

war or by special measures directed towards property during time of war, the substantive part of the claim will have been proved. In determining the type of proof necessary, the particular standards set forth in applicable treaties and statutes should be consulted, but generally war claims are prepared in the same manner as claims for wrongs against persons or wrongs to interests in property.

CHAPTER V

The Preparation of an
International Claim: Damages

DAMAGES in an international claim are ascertained by the measurable pecuniary loss sustained by the injured party.[255] This measure serves as a convenient rule both when a claim is espoused by the United States as its own or when it is presented by the claimant to the Foreign Claims Settlement Commission distributing funds under a lump sum settlement. In a recent Department of State memorandum, a caution is sounded against the submission of claims in exaggerated amounts:

> So far as concerns the amount of damages or losses claimed, it should be observed that the making of claims in exaggerated amounts, which cannot be substantiated by satisfactory evidence or otherwise justified, usually has a prejudicial effect and should, therefore, be avoided.[256]

[255] 5 HACKWORTH 718–21.
[256] See Appendix C.

As in an action before municipal courts, evidence supporting the demand for damages should be gathered as soon as possible in order to preserve its credibility and probative value. Three types of damage are sufficiently different to warrant detailed treatment: (1) personal injury and death; (2) loss of or damage to property; and (3) breach or repudiation of contract or concession. In addition, certain special aspects of damages will be discussed at the chapter's end.

Personal Injury and Wrongful Death Claims

1. *Personal Injury Claims.* A claimant should list in his statement of claim his damages resulting from personal injuries. These damages may include physical injury to body [257] and mind,[258] injuries sustained during a period of unlawful detention,[259] measurable loss resulting from undue interference with personal liberty,[260] and any other measurable loss caused by personal injuries constituting an international wrong. Damage is computed both from out-of-pocket expenses directly related to the injury, from expected future expenses, and from prospective as well as past losses based upon impairment of earning capacity.[261] Genuine injury to the claimant's business [262] or reputation [263] may also be included if it can be measured. The Foreign Claims Settlement

[257] 1 WHITEMAN 519.

[258] *Id.* at 531, 561, 580–81, 588, 593. "Damages are not allowed for mental suffering, shock, grief, worry, and the like, where there is no attendant personal injury or pecuniary loss." *Id.* at 627.

[259] See comparative tables for damages for short and long periods of detention, *Id.* at 385–408.

[260] 5 HACKWORTH 745.

[261] *Id.* at 742; 1 WHITEMAN 594.

[262] *Id.* at 537.

[263] *Id.* at 259. *But see Id.* at 292 (reasonable grounds for detention precludes damages for injury to reputation resulting therefrom).

Commission established a schedule for use in the Italian claims program whereby appropriate compensation for various personal injury and death claims was arbitrarily fixed.[264]

Actual out-of-pocket expenses incurred up to the time a claim is prepared are documented by certified copies of receipts, bills, correspondence, and other statements regarding expenses. Hospital costs, physicians' fees, drug bills, and costs for nursing care and other personal services necessitated by the injury are proved in the same way. If transportation is a major expense, as it would be in taking an injured party to another place or country for special treatment, a medical opinion should support the itemized expenditures.

Other actual losses which can be ascertained with certainty are wages lost while the claimant is absent from gainful employment and other direct losses sustained by reason of the inability of the claimant to attend to his normal duties.[265] Loss of wages is proved through affidavits from employers regarding lost time and earning capacity. Loss of business is more difficult to establish because it requires evidence proving either the loss of business profits or the expenses incurred in hiring persons to assume business responsibilities while the claimant is incapacitated. For example, if a loss results from a claimant's inability to conclude an imminent sale to an already willing buyer (which must be established by credible evidence), then the amount of the commission reflected in the broker's contract could be considered as an out-of-pocket expense. Costs of replacement or repair of clothes, personal property affected by the wrong, and necessary services with respect thereto also should be itemized and supported by receipts, bills, or canceled checks.

Although actual expenses can be proved with some degree of certainty, future medical, hospital, and other similar expenses

[264] FCSC 1959 REP. 142.
[265] 1 WHITEMAN 598.

must be estimated, preferably by the expert opinion of the physician who has personal knowledge of the extent of the injuries and the approximate cost of future treatment. Future expenses are not disallowed merely because they are prospective, although they must not be too remote or inconsequential. A physician's statement in affidavit form might also include other estimates of damage, such as future transportation expenses, costs for personal care, and reasonable expenses for drugs and supplies.

The extent of injuries and any resulting physical suffering also should be established by a sworn statement by the physician treating the injured person. The physician should provide a full report with a diagnosis and a summary of the treatment taken and the necessary future treatment. In such a statement all elements of damage within the special knowledge of the physician should be included, such as future medical expenses and future temporary or permanent disability. A physician's estimate of the physical and mental suffering in monetary terms should be given in this report in order to support the allegation of the amount of compensation requested in the statement of claim. Demonstrative evidence, such as duly authenticated photographs or colored slides, will corroborate and lend weight to the physician's statement.

At least part of the proof needed to established the claimant's loss of future income can be supplied in the statement by his physician, which should include an assessment of the effects of the injury on the claimant's future capacity to earn money and may be expressed in percentage terms. While a medical opinion may set the percentage of permanent or temporary impairment of future earning capacity, the actual present earning capacity at the time of injury and any increases that could have been expected should be established by means of an affidavit from the claimant's employer or the submission of business records of the injured party. The age of the claimant, together with properly identified actuarial tables, should be used to compute loss of partial earning capacity based on a work life expectancy. The future loss should be capitalized to present value.

While not excluded as a matter of law, punitive damages based upon aggravated assaults or grave injustices are rarely allowed.[266] Consequently, any basis for punitive damages should be documented extensively with sworn statements of independent witnesses and convincing evidence illustrating willful or wanton misconduct on the part of foreign officials.

2. *Wrongful Death Claims*. A claim for wrongful death accrues to the survivors of the decedent rather than to his estate.[267] The umpire of the United States and German Mixed Claims Commission set out in the famous *Lusitania* cases a formula which is still very useful in computing compensation for wrongful deaths:

> Estimate the amounts (a) which the decedent, had he not been killed, would probably have contributed to the claimant, add thereto (b) the pecuniary value to such claimant of the deceased's personal services in claimant's care, education, or supervision, and also add (c) reasonable compensation for such mental suffering or shock, if any, caused by the violent severing of family ties, as claimant may actually have sustained by reason of such death. The sum of these estimates, reduced to its present cash value, will generally represent the loss sustained by claimant.[268]

Implicit in the above formula is damage for "the deprivation of personal companionship and cherished associations consequent

---

[266] *Id.* at 722. See also note 270 *infra* (punitive damages not computed in certain war claims following World War I).

[267] See text at note 173 *supra*.

[268] 5 HACKWORTH 749–50.

upon the loss of a husband or wife unexpectedly taken away." [269]

The amount of financial support which the decedent would have contributed to the claimant is established by evidence of the relationship of the two, the age of the deceased at the time of his death, the deceased's life expectancy (by actuarial tables) and his expected income (by statements of employer, income patterns, rank and position, and statements by business or professional associates regarding his future potential), together with an estimate of the percentage of the deceased's income that would have gone to the claimant had the death not occurred.[270] Dam-

[269] RALSTON, VENEZUELAN ARBITRATIONS OF 1903 769 (1904).

[270] In the opinion in the *Lusitania* cases, the following factors were enumerated as bearing on estimates of damages for wrongful death:

"(a) the age, sex, health, condition and station in life, occupation, habits of industry and sobriety, mental and physical capacity, frugality, earning capacity and customary earnings of the deceased and the uses made of such earnings by him;

"(b) the probable duration of the life of deceased but for the fatal injury, in arriving at which standard life-expectancy tables and all other pertinent evidence offered will be considered;

"(c) the reasonable probability that the earning capacity of deceased, had he lived, would either have increased or decreased;

"(d) the age, sex, health, condition and station in life, and probable life expectancy of each of the claimants;

"(e) the extent to which the deceased, had he lived, would have applied his income from his earnings or otherwise to his personal expenditures from which claimants would have derived no benefits;

"(f) in reducing to their present cash value contributions which would probably have been made from time to time to claimants by deceased, a 5% interest rate and standard present-value tables will be used;

"(g) neither the physical pain nor the mental anguish which the *deceased* may have suffered will be considered as elements of damage;

"(h) the amount of insurance on the life of the deceased collected by his estate or by the claimants will not be taken into account in computing the damages which claimants may be entitled to recover;

"(i) no exemplary, punitive, or vindictive damages can be assessed."

5 HACKWORTH 750. See also the suggestions by the Department of State, Appendix C.

ages for the loss of the decedent's personal services is established by affidavits of the claimant, others with personal knowledge of the extent and value of decedent's services, and estimates by qualified persons of personal care and similar items of expense. Reasonable compensation for mental suffering, shock, or loss of companionship may be estimated by medical opinion.

Expenses of the estate of the deceased incurred as a result of the wrongful death may be claimed by his executor or administrator, or by the heirs and legatees if paid by them.[271] Medical, hospital, and perhaps funeral expenses may be included and can be established by receipts, bills, statements, or correspondence. Where an executor or administrator is not one of the survivors of the deceased, the separate claim brought on behalf of the estate may be joined with the claim of the decedent's survivors. Most claims for wrongful death will be presented to the Department of State, since the Foreign Claims Settlement Commission, with one possible exception,[272] has not been given jurisdiction to decide death claims.[273]

Loss of or Damage to Property

Unless otherwise provided by agreement or statute, the computation of damages for loss of or damage to property or interests in property is based upon the value of the property at the time it was taken or destroyed, or upon the difference in value of the property before and after the damage occurred.[274] In estab-

[271] 1 WHITEMAN 789.

[272] FCSC 1959 REP. 139–42, 160–61 (claims against Italy under the Lombardo Agreement of 1947).

[273] *Id.* at 40–41.

[274] FCSC 1955 REP. 196, indicating the general rule of value at the time of taking but also explaining the use of prewar value in claims arising against Yugoslavia after World War II: "[1938] was the last year, prior to the takings, in which economic conditions and the resulting price and

lishing the value of property nationalized or taken by foreign countries, however, the claimant is confronted with the problem of obtaining reliable evidence. He may consider "purchase price, age and condition of the property, appraisals by experts and by individuals having personal knowledge of the facts, as well as rental income and values determined for similar types of property in the same or adjacent areas." [275] But how does the claimant go about securing such evidence?

1. *Property Loss.* A total loss of property may result either from total destruction or from a taking by a foreign country under nationalization laws, eminent domain statutes, or similar procedures. In most cases the measure of damages is the value of the property at the time of loss, plus interest to the date of the award. Value means the reasonable or fair market value of the property.[276]

Evidence probative of value includes contracts, deeds, vouch-

---

value structure were still comparatively 'normal,' as compared with the inflation, and at times extreme fluctuation and even chaos, that set in with the realization in Yugoslavia of the imminence of war beginning in 1939, and its actuality in 1941 and thereafter. Values as of 1938 were used, in short, because it was regarded as the last year for which it was practicable to determine values for the property concerned, and because the time allowed for the determination of claims and the funds available for that purpose did not permit an exhaustive investigation of claims on an individual basis." See also 2 WHITEMAN 1085.

[275] FCSC 1959 REP. 43, stating that in view of difficulties in proving valuation the Commission "made independent investigations in an effort to assist claimants."

[276] *Id.* at 198; 5 HACKWORTH 758–60 (both "reasonable" and "fair" market value used interchangeably). Whiteman concludes: "When the market value of realty is referred to, usually various elements are, or may be, comprehended, such as its tax value, its last sale value, its mortgage value, the sales value of other more or less similar realty, the condition of realty at the time of sale, the condition of the industry for which it is intended to use the realty, its adaptability for use in this particular industry, etc.; these and many other considerations may enter into the final determination of market value." 2 WHITEMAN 1547.

ers, and tax rolls showing the original cost of the property plus the nature and cost of subsequent improvements; the amount of mortgages or encumbrances on the property; the amount the property has depreciated; appraisals by qualified experts who are familiar with the general market value of property in the area; book value of business or corporate property; studies and reports by industrial engineers; and affidavits of persons with special knowledge of the reasonable value of the property at the time of loss. Photographs, extracts from corporate books, accountants' reports, measurements and statistics of industrial capacity and physical plant, income derived from the property for several years previous, and other facts establishing special circumstances will corroborate an expert's estimate of the fair market value. Evidence of inventories, accounts, and other supplies on hand also should be furnished.[277]

When a market value is impossible to prove because a radical change has occurred in the economy of a country or for some other reason, alternative methods of valuation must be used. These methods vary from simple valuations based on insurance appraisals or tax assessments to complex computations of the going concern value of industrial property, containing such factors as replacement or reproduction cost at a particular time, corporate income (both gross and net) as indicated in the profit and loss statements or tax reports, past production statistics and schedules, item by item lists of machinery fixtures, and engineering studies. No simple standard for arriving at value in the absence of a free market has been found, although the effect of several different methods of valuation seems to be quantitative or cumulative. Thus, when one or more method for valuing property is submitted in evidence, a greater probability exists that an adequate award will be made. Often it is too costly, however, to submit several different expert appraisals based on different methods.

[277] See Appendix D.

Moreover, even if all available methods are used in the documentation of a claim for damages, no single criterion exists for deciding what weight should be given to each. Much depends on variables such as the background of the claims commissioners or government officials handling the claim. These people should be consulted before preparing any one type of damage estimate.

Using "book value" [278] or inferring the value of property from corporate books reflecting net and gross income, expenses, depreciation schedules, or profit and loss statements always raises questions if two sets of books have been kept: one for the foreign authorities and one for the corporation's home office. The weight which should be given to "book value" might depend on whether a corporation could convince the Department of State or the Foreign Claims Settlement Commission that keeping two sets of books should not cast doubt on the credibility of both. In the past the practice has been justified upon the ground that this was the customary way of doing business in many foreign countries. Such an explanation would tend to lend greater weight to the books in the home office, which are presumably a more accurate reflection of the value of the property. The Department or Commission may wonder, however, whether or not a third, still more accurate set of books might not exist. If such a doubt is unrequited, it may result in less weight being given to the home office books which have been produced.

Under provisions contained in certain executive agreements, the Foreign Claims Settlement Commission frequently assists claimants in proving valuation by employing experts to make actual on-the-spot investigations at the location of former houses, businesses, land, or industrial sites and to furnish written ap-

---

[278] See, for example, the computation of value of corporate property, including debts, formerly owned by the Singer Manufacturing Company and taken by the Soviet Government or its predecessor. FCSC 1959 REP. 263–73.

praisals of their value. The Protocol with Poland of November 29, 1960,[279] which implemented Article V of the 1960 claims agreement,[280] spelled out a working arrangement for obtaining evidence in Poland when requested by representatives of the Commission. Documentary evidence proving the value of the property, as well as its ownership and present status, could be requested. Under the Protocol, Polish experts also may provide information on prewar value of arable and forest land of various classes and regions, statistical information on value of typical urban and rural dwellings, and similar data concerning small industrial and commercial enterprises. Such statistical information is very helpful in overcoming problems of proof. Physical inspections of property by United States representatives, made in the presence of Polish officials, also are permitted upon written request. Such inspections make it unnecessary to rely upon secondary evidence, often used in valuing shares of stock in nationalized corporations where it is impossible to make appraisals of the corporation's assets on the spot.[281]

If a country refuses to permit physical investigations by experts or will not otherwise help American claimants to obtain evidence

[279] Protocol With Poland, Nov. 29, 1960 [1960] 11 U.S.T. & O.I.A. 2450, T.I.A.S. No. 4629.

[280] Agreement With Poland, July 16, 1960 [1960] 11 U.S.T. & O.I.A. 1954, T.I.A.S. No. 4545.

[281] "In computing the values of the shares of stock of Rumanian corporations at the time of their nationalization, it being impossible to make on-the-spot appraisals, the Commission has considered quotations on various European stock exchanges, financial data from Compass and other publications, balance sheets and operating statements, book values and advice obtained from governmental and financial sources in foreign countries, as well as information provided by various claimants with respect to prices paid for the shares of stock and their values. On the basis of all the evidence and information available, the Commission . . ." ascertained the value of shares of stock. FCSC 1959 REP. 120. See also Id. at 68 and FCSC 1955 REP. 197–99.

in support of their claims, the Commission has been faced with a dilemma: should it reject such claims for failure to meet the burden of proof? should it give some weight to self-serving, uncorroborated evidence? or should it recognize some presumption or inference sufficient to meet the burden of proof and support an award? If awards are made on the basis of uncorroborated evidence or presumptions, payments to claimants with adequate proof might be diminished, since all claimants share proportionately in the distribution of the available claims fund. Moreover, an incentive is added thereby for exaggerating the value of a claim in order not to be penalized for being honest. The dilemma is heightened because claimants with adequate evidence are often large corporations, while needy persons with smaller claims possess inadequate evidence.

The increased use of experts and accumulated statistics to establish general standards for valuing particular kinds of property is one way to help reduce disparate results. A second method is to increase the responsibilities of the Commission in obtaining evidence through its own sources. A third solution, at least for future claims programs, is to encourage private persons to keep adequate records and proper accounts of property abroad, as well as to use private ingenuity in obtaining evidence from such countries. In distributing the lump sum which the United States received from Turkey in 1934, the American commissioner viewed the problem in the following terms:

> *Compensation* may be estimated, although it cannot be computed with absolute certainty, but it cannot be fixed solely on a basis of conjecture. In spite of uncertainty of the record as to the *character and value* of property destroyed, by resorting to very liberal practice some compensation may be made.[282]

[282] NIELSEN, AMERICAN-TURKISH CLAIMS SETTLEMENT, OPINIONS AND REPORT 272 (1937).

The Foreign Claims Settlement Commission, in attempting to meet this problem, has gone well beyond the above approach by rendering awards (albeit in reduced amounts) when there has been an "absence of reliable evidence" regarding the *ownership* as well as the *value* of the property taken.[283]

2. *Property Damage.* Since the measure of damages for loss of value of property, when the loss is less than total, is the difference in value before and after damage, a claimant must establish property value both at the time immediately preceding the wrongful act and immediately thereafter. The former can be shown by proving the purchase price of the property, as evidenced by contracts, deeds, receipts, and land records, or by furnishing an independent appraised market value by an expert. The value of property after damage should be estimated by an expert, if possible, who should include in his affidavit the basis for his evaluation. If it is impossible to prove market value, the cost of repair is a good measure of damage. Other evidence might consist of before and after photographs, carefully itemized statements of personal property damaged and the estimated value thereof, original acquisition or construction costs, documented costs of repairs and improvements before damage, and affidavits of persons with personal knowledge of the property who are in a position to know the nature and amount of damage to it.[284]

[283] FCSC 1959 REP. 21, 68, 121. In the Niagara Shore Corporation claim, the Commission said: "Claimant has been unable to submit evidence which fully substantiates its allegations as to the extent of the loss with respect to these shares of stock. Nevertheless, the Commission, not being bound by the usual rules of evidence, is persuaded that the claimant owned stock interests in said corporations which were taken within the meaning of Section 303(2) of the Act, apparently in 1948, and that no compensation has been paid therefor by the Government of Rumania. Denial of the claim for lack of corroboration under such circumstances, would not, in the opinion of the Commission, be an act of justice. On the other hand, the absence of reliable evidence precludes an award of the full amount claimed." *Id.* at 121. See note 185 *supra*.

[284] See Appendix D.

A problem in valuation of damages occurs when interference with property is not such that it is considered to be an effective taking for which full value must be paid. If possession of occupied property is restored, for instance, then the measure of damage is the fair rental value for the time it was used plus any reduction in its value.[285] If rents set by a foreign country are nominal or inadequate, other evidence for proving fair rental value can be used, such as rents previously received and the reasonable return on property of the type involved.

Breach or Repudiation of Contract or Concession

Ideally, damages flowing from international wrongs involving contracts should place the injured party in a position comparable to that which he would have been in had no wrong taken place or had the contract been performed. A wrong to interests in a contract may amount to a taking of the contract itself, similar to the taking of property considered above,[286] or it may be a breach of the contract accompanied by the failure of a country to provide a remedy for damages.[287] More often, in recent cases involving international contracts or concession agreements, the wrong is something less than the taking of the contract and something more than a mere breach. For example, an oil concession may be canceled in part for nonproducing areas or legislation may be passed restricting profits or unilaterally increasing a foreign country's royalties.

In any wrong involving a contract, certified copies of the contract documents themselves should accompany proof of damage. If the wrong is based upon an alleged breach of the contract,

---

[285] 5 HACKWORTH 761.
[286] See note 244 *supra.*
[287] See text at notes 241–42 *supra.*

damages are computed on the loss of nonspeculative profits (*lucrum cessans*) established by such evidence as business records, market statistics, or expert opinion. Any other direct, measurable loss regarded as special damages or out-of-pocket expenses may also be claimed (*dammum emergens*). If the wrong is based upon an annulment or repudiation of the contract, the measure of damages is the value of the contract itself established by such evidence as book value, appraisals by experts using the analytical or engineering method and receipts for expenditures made in reliance on the contract. Evidence of past profits such as certified statements of profit and loss also can be useful in supporting the value placed on the contract.

If in reliance on a contract an American national invests money abroad for the purpose of drilling oil or mining subsurface minerals, and the foreign government repudiates the contract, the value of the benefits unjustly retained by the country would be considered in the amount claimed. Benefits would include expenditures incurred, services performed, supplies furnished, or work and labor done.[288]

In proving the value of a concession agreement, the amount of future profits is always uncertain to a degree. Furthermore, the value of the contract itself might be measured in many different ways. For example, the value of untapped mineral reserves of unknown extent in a concession area might be shown by submitting independent surveys of engineers, geophysicists, or geologists, which estimate the value of the minerals, the cost of extracting them, and the expected market price.[289] Another measure

[288] 3 WHITEMAN 1746–61.

[289] FCSC 1955 REP. 166. Evidence included "production and income statistics for the years 1926–30, and the affidavits of the former quarry manager and a Yugoslav mining engineer as to the annual rate of production, the amount of marble unquarried, past profits and estimated value of the concession." In addition, evidence was filed as to the estimated annual net income for the remaining life of the concession.

of damages would be the worth of the concession itself on the "market," which would take into account not only the unexplored or untapped oil or mineral reserves, as indicated by geological reports, but also the value of the reserves capitalized to the present time based upon depreciation schedules or as reflected in the net worth of the company.[290]

Although bonds are contracts, the Department of State does not generally make a practice of espousing claims based on defaulted bonds of foreign governments.[291] However, under international agreements and domestic legislation, claims for defaulted bonds have sometimes been paid.[292] Bondholder claims also may be compensable if they are based on outright cancellation or repudiation.[293] If the Department of State ever sought to obtain the full par value of repudiated bonds when the claimants had acquired them at great discounts, an inequity would exist that would be hard to justify. Accordingly, some evidence of acquisition cost should be submitted, such as affidavits, receipts, or canceled checks. The Foreign Claims Settlement Commission, under domestic legislation, has refused to render awards in ex-

[290] FCSC 1959 REP. 130. In estimating the value of oil reserves, the analytical or engineering method of appraisal was used. "In applying the method claimant has assumed that all of the leases are valid, has used prewar cost experience 'adjusted' to 1948, has figured sales prices on the basis of a competitive free market and projected these costs and prices over the years to 1978 and 1983. Additionally, the claimant has assumed, for the remaining life of the leases, a government tax of 50% plus 11% royalty." *Ibid.* While the Commission recognized the validity of the method, it was not convinced that the assumptions were correct. "In arriving at the market value at the date of nationalization, the Commission is not presently convinced that a buyer in a competitive market would be willing to pay the figure asserted by the claimant." *Ibid.* Accordingly, the Commission reduced the award by an undisclosed discount.

[291] 5 HACKWORTH 611, 625–26.

[292] *E.g.,* 69 Stat. 571 (1955), 22 U.S.C. § 1641b (1958).

[293] FCSC FOURTEENTH SEMIANN. REP. 196, implying that a property right in bonds would be taken only by repudiation or cancellation thereof.

cess of the cost of acquisition of bonds unless the claimant owned the bonds when the claim originally accrued.[294] In this case, the market value at the time of cancellation or repudiation determines damage. It is established by published market quotations, statements of brokers, average market prices, or reliable financial publications. The bonds themselves must be turned in with the statement of claim.

Special Aspects of Damages

1. *Deductions.* Appropriate deductions should be made for amounts obtained through local remedies in foreign countries.[295] Generally, a statement by a claimant and a certified copy of any award or decision will show the extent to which he has been compensated by an action abroad, whether administrative or judicial. If no compensation has been obtained in a foreign country, a claimant should include that fact in his statement of claim.

Although encumbrances of insignificant amounts are often disregarded in determining the amount of an award for the taking of property,[296] the Foreign Claims Settlement Commission will make appropriate deductions for unsatisfied mortgages,[297] taxes payable,[298] outstanding judgments,[299] and life estates and remainder interests.[300] The Department of State takes the same approach.

[294] FCSC 1959 Rep. 201.

[295] *Cf.* FCSC 1955 Rep. 60–61. A stockholder's claim for damages was reduced when his corporation, a British concern, received an award from the British Foreign Compensation Commission. *Id.* at 61–62. *Cf.* FCSC 1959 Rep. 25–26.

[296] FCSC 1955 Rep. 199–200.

[297] *Id.* at 202–03.

[298] *Id.* at 200, 211.

[299] *Id.* at 201.

[300] *Id.* at 201–02.

In preparing a claim for submission either to the Department or the Commission, the claimant should submit documentary evidence about amounts of insurance he has received as a result of the international wrong.[301] Whether insurance proceeds (and paid premiums) will be taken into account in computing a claimant's damages today is unclear. Much would depend upon the nature and amount of the insurance, as well as the claims program involved.[302]

A final problem in this area arises when an uncompensated loss based upon an international wrong has been deducted by a claimant from income on his United States tax return on the ground that it was a business loss. The Foreign Claims Settlement Commission will not deduct the amount of the resulting tax benefit from a subsequent award unless required to do so by statute.[303] Since the Department of State in obtaining settlement of a claim which it is espousing has discretionary control over the claim, it could subtract the amount of tax benefit received by the claimant either before the claim is presented or after an award has been paid to the United States. The latter alternative would permit the United States taxpayers to recoup the loss shared by all through the means of a tax write-off.

2. *Costs.* Although expenses in preparing the international claim itself must be borne by the claimant and may not be computed in damages asked,[304] the cost of exhausting local remedies is a justified item of damage.[305] Prior expenses include court costs, attorneys' fees, and necessary travel costs. They can be estab-

[301] See Appendix D and Item No. 17(b) of Form No. 709, Appendix B.
[302] Proposed legislation providing for the payment of German War Claims requires the Foreign Claims Settlement Commission to deduct, among other items, insurance monies. See Section 206 of H.R. 7479, 87th Cong., 1st Sess. (1961).
[303] FCSC 1959 REP. 214–15. See note 302 *supra.*
[304] *Id.* at 58–60, 125, 245.
[305] 3 WHITEMAN 2020–28 *passim.*

lished by affidavits, receipts, and certified court records.[306]

3. *Interest.* Interest on the amount claimed is generally computed from the date of the taking of property by a foreign country at least to the date of settlement.[307] Interest on awards for personal injury or wrongful death, since it is generally not itemized separately, is normally considered within the amount of general damages requested.[308] When interest is allowed the rate is usually six per cent.[309]

4. *Currency Problems.* A claim for compensation for loss or damage should be made in terms of United States dollars. Normally it is computed in the foreign currency at the time of loss or damage and then converted into dollars at the rate of exchange available at the time the claim arose.[310] In setting a dollar value on claims the Foreign Claims Settlement Commission generally compiles tables for converting foreign currency into dollars.[311] The tables list rates of exchange for certain periods of time covering the approximate time during which the international wrongs occurred.

A question might arise whether the imposition of foreign exchange controls on currency an American has abroad is a basis for an international claim. In the context of possible Cuban claims, the Department of State recently stated the widely held view that:

> As a general rule, a limitation on the purchase of dollar exchange does not constitute a legal ground for an international claim against the Cuban Government, as it is generally ac-

---

[306] See text at note 404 *infra.*

[307] 3 WHITEMAN 1913–31. See also FCSC 1955 REP. 18–20 and FCSC 1959 REP. 89–93.

[308] 3 WHITEMAN 1984–88.

[309] See note 307 *supra.*

[310] 5 HACKWORTH 732.

[311] FCSC 1955 REP. 121–24.

cepted in international law and practice that a state has the right to regulate foreign exchange. The right to regulate does not, however, include the right to discriminate against nationals of a particular country or to deprive an owner of an account of all rights of ownership.[312]

Similarly, loss through inflation or devaluation of foreign currency may not be included in damages claimed in the absence of discriminatory treatment or effective taking.[313]

5. *Awards Exceeding Amount Claimed.* Many claimants under recent claims programs, through lack of knowledge of property values or otherwise, have understated the value of property taken by foreign countries. In such cases, the Foreign Claims Settlement Commission has not held the claimants to the amounts claimed "where the actual valuation of the property upon the evidence proves to be in excess of the amount so claimed." [314] Presumably such an approach would be taken by the Department of State, although it is more likely to occur under programs administered by the Commission, which undertakes itself to gather evidence whenever possible.

[312] Department of State Memorandum entitled "Cuban Exchange Controls," March 1, 1961, reprinted in 56 AM. J. INT'L L. 165 (1962).

[313] FCSC 1955 REP. 22, 120–25.

[314] *Id.* at 21. See also FCSC 1959 REP. 187, 212.

CHAPTER VI

The Presentation of an International Claim to the Department of State

A PERSON with a valid international claim against a foreign country should first address an informal inquiry to the Department of State concerning the appropriate procedures to be followed to obtain redress. As the Department has pointed out, it has handled such matters:

> (1) by submitting individual claims through the diplomatic channel to the foreign government concerned and obtaining restitution or compensation; (2) by obtaining a lump sum in settlement of all claims, with the amount paid distributed by an agency of the United States Government; or (3) by an agreement submitting all claims to an international arbitral tribunal for adjudication.[315]

[315] Department of State Memorandum entitled "Nationalization, Intervention or Other Taking of Property of American Nationals," March 1, 1961, reprinted in 56 AM. J. INT'L L. 166 (1962).

The first alternative, the traditional method of espousal, will be considered in this chapter, with the lump sum settlement–national commission device being stressed in the chapter to follow.

Seeking Department of State espousal of his claim is often the only remedy available to a claimant, particularly if his claim is based upon an isolated occurrence. Even when his claim is one of a group of claims eventually referred to a national or an international claims commission, the claimant may be advised to present his claim to the Department along the way. The various problems inherent in such presentation fall under the following seven headings: (1) procedural safeguards; (2) method and criteria; (3) duties of the claimant; (4) control over the claim; (5) exhaustion of local remedies; (6) assistance short of espousal; and (7) settlement and distribution.

PROCEDURAL SAFEGUARDS

Since the decision whether or not to present a formal claim to a foreign government is said to be entirely within the discretion of the Department of State,[316] claimants as a matter of right do not have access to an administrative hearing where their request for diplomatic interposition might be weighed.[317] However, in practice any claimant or his attorney may make appointments to meet with officers of the Legal Adviser's Office of the Department in order to present a claim. As no procedural rights are formalized, the validity of a claim must be demonstrated by convincing evidence presented to the Department during such meetings or by mail.

It is possible that a more formal administrative procedure for

[316] RESTATEMENT, FOREIGN RELATIONS § 217 (Proposed Official Draft, 1962); 1 WHITEMAN 164–65, 275.
[317] *Id.* at 2046.

presenting claims for espousal would increase the effectiveness of the process by safeguarding against excessive use of subjective standards by the Department in its determination of the validity of a claim for espousal purposes. At present one insurance against arbitrariness is the built-in separation of the Legal Adviser's Office from the political and other bureaus of the Department of State. Using traditional international law and practice as a starting point, the Legal Adviser's Office applies a legal method in judging the validity of claims. The safeguards to individuals offered by the function of the Legal Adviser's Office are twofold. In the first place, they may participate with legal officers in a decision-making process by presenting claims in their most favorable light. Secondly, they may rest assured that a refusal to espouse a claim for international political reasons will not occur unless the Department has determined that the force and weight of the legal opinion supporting a claim is outbalanced by other factors comprising the national interest.

Method and Criteria

Even the initial, informal presentation of a claim to the Department of State should be prepared very carefully, since at this stage the responsible officers will be objectively critical of weak points, gaps in proof, and fallacies in the theory of the claim. The purpose of meeting with legal officers in the Department or in corresponding with them should be to prove the validity of the claim so that the United States Government can give its full support to the claim by espousing it formally as though it were its own. When a person initially presents a claim, he should have prepared a concise statement of the facts and the legal basis of the claim. Such a statement of claim can be developed in detail at a later date if the Department so requests.

In deciding whether the claim is meritorious and, if so, what assistance, if any, can be provided, the Department has a dual function. Its first role is akin to that of a lawyer who must decide whether to take a client's case.[318] The reactions of the Department of State's legal officers will be similar to those of a critical lawyer who cross-examines his client to get at all the relevant facts. This comparison is somewhat limited, however, for if the Department refuses to support a claim the claimant may have no other advocate to which to turn. The Department's second role is that of the traditional advocate, which it assumes when it interposes in behalf of an injured American national. After deciding to assist the claimant, the Department has a choice of a number of various degrees of support that, while appropriate from a political point of view, ought at the same time to be productive of some relief.[319]

In deciding whether to assist a claimant, the Department uses criteria in addition to its assessment of the legal merits of the claim. These factors are generally the defenses that the foreign country could be expected to raise or the voluntary acts of the claimant by which he might have lost his right to diplomatic protection. Thus the Department considers: (1) whether the claimant violated any law in connection with his grievance;[320] (2) whether the claimant was contributorily negligent;[321] (3) whether the claimant's acts in any way justified the action by the foreign government causing him injury;[322] (4) whether an

[318] Whiteman compares this function to that of a tribunal of first instance. *Id.* at 165.

[319] In addition to espousing a formal international claim through diplomatic channels, the Department may resort to more informal means of obtaining a remedy. See text at and accompanying notes 345–48 *infra.*

[320] *Id.* at 142–46 *passim.*

[321] *Id.* at 144.

[322] RESTATEMENT, FOREIGN RELATIONS §§ 202–04 (Proposed Official Draft, 1962) (reasonable exercise of police power, currency control, and protection of life and property in case of emergency).

unreasonably long time has passed since the claim accrued, raising the possible objection of laches; [323] (5) whether the claimant has lost his right of protection by voluntary expatriation, express or implied; [324] and (6) whether the claimant has endeavored to exhaust his local remedies in the foreign country.[325]

Perhaps the most frequent objection made by the Department of State at the initial stage of presentation is the failure of the claimant to exhaust local remedies,[326] closely followed by the lack of eligibility to assert a claim.[327] Political objections to immediate presentation might also be raised. Occasionally valid claims are not presented but are preserved for future settlement. Any attempt to be objective about the procedures of the Department in determining the validity of claims must postpone the question of how international politics enters an espousal until after the legal process is completed. Assuming that a claim is judged legally sound, the chances are good that action will be taken if it is at all possible.

DUTIES OF THE CLAIMANT

Even though international claims are theoretically claims of the United States government, the responsibility for preparing and documenting them rests exclusively with the claimants. Failure to bear this responsibility may result in the denial of support for the claim. Aggrieved nationals sometimes have the mistaken view

[323] 5 HACKWORTH 713–17.

[324] *Id.* at 709–10, 802–51.

[325] *Id.* at 501–26. See text at and accompanying notes 337–43 *infra.*

[326] The latest pronouncement of this requirement is found in the Interhandel Case, [1959] I.C.J. REP. 6.

[327] Naturalized United States citizens, for instance, are turned down if their claims arose when they were foreign nationals. See text at and accompanying notes 33–36 *supra.*

that the United States will father the claim and benevolently protect American interests so long as some complaint is registered
with the Department of State.[328] This view is often prejudicial to
meritorious claims which might need only proper preparation to
warrant espousal. Claimants should be sure that they have not
been dilatory in exhausting local remedies, preserving the evidence available, or translating documents and preparing clear
statements of claim.

In dealing with the Department of State, the services of an experienced attorney are valuable but not required. Attorneys' fees
incurred in the preparation and presentation of an international
claim are borne exclusively by the claimant and may not be included in damages claimed.[329] In the course of informal dealings
with the Department a formal power of attorney may not be required, but when an attorney presents a formal claim he must file
a written power of attorney to accompany the claim.[330]

Part of a claimant's responsibility includes the preservation of
a claim during the time when a foreign country is unfriendly or
unwilling to consider settling it. Thus, making an early and complete record is particularly important in claims against countries
in foment or civil strife. Claimants are naturally discouraged from
spending time and money in preparing and documenting claims
against a country like Cuba when they discover that the only

[328] "There is an impression that it is only necessary to inform the
Department of State of the claim. But if the American client wants results within a reasonable time, his local attorney must take the initiative
and do most of the work." Cowles, *supra* note 10, at 195.

[329] 1 WHITEMAN 791; 3 WHITEMAN 2028–29. Equity and fairness have
been the basis for awarding legal expenses on occasion. *Id.* at 2026. Prior
legal expenses incurred in the exhausion of local remedies, on the other
hand, may be included as a general rule. *Id.* at 2020, 2022–23, 2026–28.
See also text at notes 304–06 *supra*.

[330] "In cases in which claimants are represented by an attorney, the
latter should file a power of attorney evidencing his authority to act in
such capacity." Appendixes C & D.

method available for presenting those claims is unlikely to be fruitful. However, the responsibility for preserving rights requires gathering evidence while it is available, presenting it to the Department of State for the record, and otherwise protecting it pending settlement.

Hundreds of claims filed with the Department at an early date have in the past been sent to the Foreign Claims Settlement Commission where they were useful in the determination of claims under the terms of lump sum agreements.[331] When legislation is eventually passed authorizing the adjudication of war damage claims against Germany and their payment from German assets vested during World War II, the records in the Department undoubtedly will be turned over to the Commission for its use.[332] In the Polish negotiations a registration of claims with the Foreign Claims Settlement Commission, an innovation in United States practice, enabled the Department, working with the Commission, to compile statistical information to support the discussions.[333]

Control Over the Claim

Prior to the espousal of a claim, the claimant himself has control over it and may negotiate a settlement directly with the

[331] During the early stages of the Yugoslav claims program, the International Claims Commission was part of the Department of State and no problem regarding the transfer of records arose. When the Commission became the Foreign Claims Settlement Commission in 1954, it was separated from the Department of State and arrangements were made for the transfer of needed records.

[332] Section 216 of the Administration's war claims bill, H.R. 7479, 87th Cong., 1st Sess. (1961), directs the Secretary of State to "transfer or otherwise make available to the Commission such records and documents relating to claims authorized by this title. . . ."

[333] LILLICH 45.

foreign country.[334] The control at this point is subject only to the possibility that the Department of State, in the exercise of its power delegated from the President, might waive or settle the claim. Should this occur, no responsibility for the taking of property falls on the United States, since international claims, for Fifth Amendment purposes, are considered to be claims of the United States. Consequently, claimants have no rights other than those procured for them by the government. However, as a matter of practice claimants generally receive their proportionate share of any settlement fund. Should an international agreement abrogate a claimant's right or interest acquired under domestic legislation, on the other hand, a duty to pay compensation under the Fifth Amendment might arise, although the Supreme Court has not yet decided this precise question.[335]

Whether to lend support to the claim of an American national by making it the claim of the United States is traditionally within the ultimate discretion of the Secretary of State. A claimant cannot compel espousal and, as mentioned above, has no right to be accorded a formal hearing on his claim. Once the Department of State espouses a claim, it acquires exclusive control over it both under traditional international law and United States practice. Consequently, it may waive or settle the claim without the claimant's consent.[336] Thus the claimant, after his claim is adopted by the United States, theoretically has little or no control over it. However, except in unusual circumstances, the Department will give great weight to the wishes of the claimant.

[334] RESTATEMENT, FOREIGN RELATIONS § 216 (Proposed Official Draft, 1962).

[335] See, generally, LILLICH 23–40.

[336] 1 WHITEMAN 275; 3 WHITEMAN 2035, 2046–47. See note 335 *supra*.

Exhaustion of Local Remedies

Before the Department of State will consider espousing a claim under principles of international law, it must be satisfied that the condition precedent of the exhaustion of local remedies has been met by the claimant.[337] Although this requirement should be alleged as one of the points in the statement of claim,[338] it is viewed here as a procedural requirement rather than as a substantive element of the claim itself.[339] The local remedies rule is so well established that the International Court of Justice, in the *Interhandel Case*, declared:

> The rule that local remedies must be exhausted before international proceedings may be instituted is a well-established rule of customary international law; the rule has been generally observed in cases in which a State has adopted the cause of its national whose rights are claimed to have been disregarded in another State in violation of international law. Before resort may be had to an international court in such a situation, it has been considered necessary that the State where the violation occurred should have an opportunity to redress it by its own means, within the framework of its own domestic legal system.[340]

---

[337] 5 Hackworth 501, 505.

[338] It can be placed either in the eligibility section or the wrongful act section of the statement of claim; it also may be stated separately. See, generally, Restatement, Foreign Relations §§ 211–15 (Proposed Official Draft, 1962).

[339] Restatement, Foreign Relations § 211, comment f at 716 (Proposed Official Draft, 1962).

[340] Interhandel Case [1959], I.C.J. Rep. 6, 27.

The most recent pronouncement by the Department of State on the local remedies rule follows in general fashion this traditional view:

> The requirement for exhaustion of local remedies is based upon the generally accepted rule of international law that international responsibility may not be invoked as regards reparation for losses or damages sustained by a foreigner until after exhaustion of the remedies available under local law. This, of course, does not mean that "legal remedies" must be exhausted if there are none to exhaust or if the procurement of justice would be impossible. . . . Each American national must . . . decide whether to "exhaust legal remedies" in Cuba, either with a view to obtaining restitution or adequate compensation or documentary evidence which could be used to show that justice could not be obtained by judicial proceedings. Generally, unsupported assertions to the effect that it would be useless to exhaust or attempt to exhaust legal remedies would, of course, have less evidentiary value than a court decree or other documentary evidence demonstrating the futility of exhausting or attempting to exhaust legal remedies.[341]

The customary international law rule regarding local remedies grew up in an age when claims were few in number and when countries had a common interest in respecting and preserving the integrity of every other country. In some respects, changed political and economic conditions have modified the assumptions underlying the traditional view. The local remedies rule would serve no purpose at all today with respect to communist countries, which would use it as a weapon to delay international discussions of claims. Nor would its purpose be served when an

[341] Department of State Memorandum entitled "Nationalization, Intervention or Other Taking of Property of American Nationals," March 1, 1961, reprinted in 56 AM. J. INT'L L. 167 (1962).

underdeveloped country unable to pay claims is involved. Thus the rule's rationale seems pertinent today only with regard to Western-oriented countries which continue to respect each other as political units and which have the resources to compensate claimants.

With the above in mind, the increasing United States practice has been to negotiate lump sum settlements of claims of American nationals without requiring the exhaustion of local remedies.[342] While such settlements recently have involved communist countries, underdeveloped or nonaligned nations needing assistance from the United States may well wish to agree to compensate Americans for any property expropriated in order to clear the way for United States aid.[343] Here again the exhaustion of local remedies might be waived. Hence, with the exception of claims based upon isolated occurrences, the trend today seems to be away from the strict enforcement of the traditional local remedies rule.

Assistance Short of Espousal

If the Department of State may refuse to present a valid international claim for political reasons, even though the claim is

[342] The lump sum agreements with Yugoslavia, Rumania and Poland, made after World War II, did not mention local remedies. Compare, however, the Department of State's position with respect to Cuban claims, text at note 341 *supra*. See Foreign Assistance Act of 1962, § 301(d)(2)(3), 76 Stat. 260 (1962).

[343] In the case of the expropriation of a utility company by Brazil in early 1962, a joint communiqué was issued by President Kennedy and President Goulart wherein the latter expressed the "intention of his government to maintain conditions of security which will permit private capital to perform its vital role in Brazilian economic development." He also stated that arrangements would be made with companies for "fair compensation with reinvestment in other sectors important to Brazilian economic development. . . ." The communiqué noted that "President Kennedy expressed great interest in this approach." 108 Cong. Rec. 5632 (daily ed. April 5, 1962).

legally valid, is the implication true that for equally cogent political reasons it could raise a claim with a foreign government when
a claimant does not have a valid claim under traditional international law? What precludes the United States from insisting, in
a politically expedient case, that a certain claim must be satisfied
without regard to traditional rules regarding local remedies or
eligibility? While the answer obviously is that nothing prevents
the United States from raising such matters politically, legal defenses developed through custom over many years undoubtedly
would be raised against a demarche of that kind.

A traditional distinction usually has been drawn between informal good offices on the political level and the more juridical
concept of formal diplomatic espousal. One international lawyer
has remarked, however, that "the difference between 'good offices' and 'diplomatic intervention' is not impressive." [344] Many
shades and variations of "informal good offices" short of formal
espousal can be requested of the Department of State. These
methods, not quite juridical or formal in nature, may be classified
according to the degree of support desired: (1) information regarding local remedies; (2) consular services; [345] (3) good offices; [346] (4) mediation; [347] and finally (5) political intervention.[348]

Frequently an embassy abroad can ascertain that there are rem-

[344] Schwebel, *International Protection of Contractual Arrangements*,
1959 PROC. AM. SOC'Y INT'L L. 266, 267.

[345] Notarial services, administration of estates, assistance to seamen,
and protection of rights of imprisoned citizens are examples of such
services. 4 HACKWORTH 824–76, 912–47.

[346] No difference in method is perceived between good offices when a
dispute exists between two governments and good offices when a dispute arises between a foreign government and an American national. 6
HACKWORTH 24; Schwebel, note 344 *supra*.

[347] Mediation is different from good offices only in degree. 6 HACK-
WORTH 24–26.

[348] Political interests involve United States interests which in a sense
are different from private interests. If a government considers its own

edies available for particular wrongs if a claimant is unable to obtain that information by his own efforts. For example, a claimant might need simply to be placed in contact with the proper officials in order to begin negotiations on a settlement of his claim. A request for information regarding remedies normally is the kind of help a United States mission abroad can honor without much objection if help cannot otherwise be obtained. Slightly more work is involved when consular services available to an American abroad are sought in connection with a claim. These services normally include furnishing lists of local lawyers, ascertaining the current status of a claim pending before local authorities, indicating to local officials the American interest involved in a particular case, and the performance of certain estate, notarial, or protection services in the event of death, imprisonment, or misfortune abroad.

Good offices in its narrow sense is concerned with arranging procedures for the settlement of a claim but not with its substantive merits. For instance, a claimant might wish to request the Department of State to instruct an embassy abroad to approach a foreign government for the purpose of bringing the parties together to negotiate a settlement. Somewhat different in degree from good offices is the device of mediation, which is used when the United States wishes to take a more active part in any negotiations, even to the extent of suggesting a compromise while at the same time avoiding a position on the merits of the claim. Finally, in cases of very great importance, interposition might take place in which United States representatives could suggest a politically desirable, substantive settlement of a particular case without regard to its legal merits.

---

interests injured, the traditional rules of state responsibility for injury to aliens might not apply, since the matter is intergovernmental from the outset.

A claimant who knows precisely what he is requesting the Department of State to do stands a better chance of accomplishing his objectives than the claimant who does not spell out the assistance he wants. Thus, if a claimant who has made a contract with a foreign country asks the Department to demand full compensation for him based upon the breach of the contract, without explaining what remedies he has sought on his own behalf, he is likely to receive a negative response. If, in the same situation, he makes a more modest request for assistance in determining what, if any, remedial procedures are available in the foreign country or which office of the foreign government handles claims administratively, he is more likely to find a sympathetic attitude, especially if he cannot obtain the information through his own means. Similarly, if a recently naturalized citizen requests support for a claim arising prior to his naturalization, he would be politely turned down. If he only requests help in finding a remedy abroad, however, he stands in better stead, since he is now a citizen entitled to such assistance just as any other citizen. A claimant quite profitably could request the Department's good offices in bringing it together with the foreign country for serious negotiations before resorting to local remedies. When action by a foreign country against an American interest affects vital United States interests, direct representation by the Department of State would be more likely for political reasons than where the interests affected have little connection with the national interest.

Within the Department of State, procedures for deciding the legal validity of claims are to a great extent insulated from international politics. With the increased use of informal procedures such as those discussed above, the results are bound to have some effect on traditional international law, at least as applied by the United States. Procedures developed politically, in addition to the traditional espousal of claims, may eventually be incorporated into traditional legal practice. For example, the local remedies rule, first waived in lump sum settlements, now seems to be accorded different weight in different political situations.[349] While it is much too early to generalize, the liberality accorded claimants short of espousal may someday be accepted as the norm of protection under the law of international claims.

SETTLEMENT AND DISTRIBUTION

Several notable differences exist between informal assistance to the claimant and the formal espousal of an international claim on his behalf. One lies in the legal implications of settlement. With informal assistance, the claimant retains control over his claim to the extent that he is party to any settlement with the foreign country.[350] The United States merely helps him arrange a settlement with the proper authorities or suggests possible solutions. An espousal is otherwise, for any settlement is within the complete control of the United States, which may compromise or settle the claim for less than the claimant might consider fair.[351] Another difference between informal and formal procedures is that the claimant carries the burden of substantive negotiations in cases in which the United States merely uses good offices or mediates, but when the United States makes a formal, diplomatic interposition it negotiates on the substantive merits of the claim.

When settlement with a foreign country is reached by a claimant, he receives payment directly as in any private settlement.

[349] It is too early to tell the significance of the joint Kennedy-Goulart communiqué, note 343 *supra*. While the remedies available in Brazil are entirely local, they have been made available in greater measure through the good offices of the President.

[350] RESTATEMENT, FOREIGN RELATIONS § 216 (Proposed Official Draft, 1962).

[351] RESTATEMENT, FOREIGN RELATIONS § 218 (Proposed Official Draft, 1962).

When a claim has been espoused by the United States and settlement is intergovernmental, payment is made directly to the United States Government and its discharge of the international obligation of the foreign country releases the claim. A claimant thereafter does not have any rights against the foreign government and receives from his own government an award within the discretion of the Secretary of State.[352] The determination of an award by the Secretary is final and not subject to review by the courts, except in regard to conflicting claims of ownership of the right to receive the award. If settlement is made for a large block of claims by means of a lump sum settlement, more formal procedures are prescribed for distributing the fund. At the present time the Foreign Claims Settlement Commission has authority to receive and determine claims settled by lump sum agreements and to distribute the funds among eligible claimants.[353]

[352] 3 WHITEMAN 2047.
[353] See note 424 *infra.*

CHAPTER VII

The Presentation of an International Claim to National or International Commissions

THE prior chapter, primarily concerned with the traditional method of espousal, covered the first of three methods by which claimants commonly seek redress. This chapter will consider two other methods used to compensate injured American nationals: the lump sum settlement–national commission device, which will be emphasized in some detail, and the resort to international commissions, which will be treated briefly.

NATIONAL COMMISSIONS

The ground rules for presenting claims to a national claims commission, such as the Foreign Claims Settlement Commission, are more detailed than the comparatively informal procedures by which Department of State espousal is sought. The substantive right of the claimant to share in the proceeds of the claims fund is governed by the settlement agreement itself or by implementing legislation.[354] The procedural steps whereby an eligible claimant establishes his right to an award from the fund are found, in turn, in implementing legislation and Commission rules and regulations.[355] It is to the latter that claimants and their attorneys most often refer.[356]

An individual claimant may appear before the Commission in his own behalf,[357] or he may be represented by an attorney admitted to practice law in any state or territory of the United States or the District of Columbia.[358] Partnership claims may be presented by a member of the partnership, while a corporation, trust, or association may be represented by an officer thereof.[359] Attorneys appearing for claimants are held to the usual high professional standard,[360] and their remuneration is limited in most instances to ten per cent of the total amount paid on account of the claim.[361]

[354] See, generally, LILLICH 23–28.

[355] *Id.* at 48–53.

[356] The Foreign Claims Settlement Commission has the statutory right to adopt such rules and regulations as it deems necessary. 64 Stat. 13 (1950), 22 U.S.C. § 1622(c) (1958). These rules are found in 45 C.F.R. §§ 500–01, 531 (1960).

[357] 45 C.F.R. § 500.1(a) (1960).

[358] 45 C.F.R. § 500.1(b) (1960).

[359] 45 C.F.R. § 500.1(a) (1960).

[360] 45 C.F.R. § 500.5 (1960). *Cf.* Herman v. Acheson, 108 F. Supp. 723 (D.C. 1952), *aff'd sub nom.* Herman v. Dulles, 205 F.2d 715 (D.C. Cir. 1953).

[361] 64 Stat. 15 (1950), 22 U.S.C. § 1623(f) (1958). *Cf.* 45 C.F.R. §§ 500.2–500.4 (1960). For a recent case concerning allowable fees, see Estate of Anninger, 147 N.Y.L.J. No. 113, p. 15, cols. 5–8, p. 16, cols. 1–2 (N.Y. Surr. Ct. June 12, 1962).

The first step which a claimant or his attorney takes is to file the claim with the Commission.[362] Unless prescribed by statute, the time limits for filing under the various claims programs within its jurisdiction are set by the Commission itself.[363] Claims are filed on official forms provided by the Commission upon written request.[364] All information called for by the appropriate form should be supplied, and the form should be completed and signed as directed.[365] Early filing is recommended,[366] especially where continuous nationality is required to the time of filing and a claimant's heirs or legatees are nonnationals.[367] If, in such a case, the health of the claimant is a matter of concern, some communication should be sent to the Commission to insure the preservation of the claim.[368]

The type of evidence which should be filed with the claim is similar to that requested by the Department of State. The Commission may subpoena witnesses and documents[369] and order

[362] Notice to the Commission, the Department of State or any other United States agency, prior to the enactment of a statute authorizing a claims program or the effective date of a lump sum settlement, of an intention to file a claim is not considered as timely filing. 45 C.F.R. § 531.2(e) (Supp. 1962). See note 366 *infra*.

[363] *Cf.* 45 C.F.R. § 531.1 (Supp. 1962).

[364] A copy of the official form for a Claim Against the Government of Poland (Form No. 709) is found in Appendix B. Forms may be obtained by writing to the Foreign Claims Settlement Commission, Washington 25, D.C.

[365] 45 C.F.R. § 531.2(a) (1960).

[366] Gillilland, *The Foreign Claims Settlement Commission*, 11 ABA INT'L & COMP. L. BULL. No. 2 at 12, 19 (1957).

[367] See note 160 *supra*.

[368] A letter to the Commission indicating an intention to file a claim, which is received within thirty days prior to the expiration of the filing period, is treated as timely filing if formalized within thirty days after the expiration date. 45 C.F.R. § 531.2(f) (Supp. 1962). See note 362 *supra*.

[369] 64 Stat. 14 (1950), 22 U.S.C. § 1623(c) (1958). See also 45 C.F.R. §§ 501.2–501.3 (1960).

depositions to be taken.[370] Documentary evidence [371] should be filed with and at the same time as the claim.[372] Whenever possible, original documents should be submitted, but copies of originals certified as such by their custodians also are permitted.[373] Each copy of a document, exhibit, or paper filed, if in a language other than English, must be accompanied by an English translation thereof duly verified under oath by its translator to be a true and accurate translation.[374] The name and address of the translator must be given as well.[375] All claims, briefs, and memoranda filed with the Commission must be typewritten on legal size paper or printed.[376]

The Commission, upon receipt of the claim, will notify the claimant in writing of the claim number assigned to his claim, which number should be used on all further correspondence and papers filed with regard to the claim.[377] The claim is then assigned to a staff attorney for study, development, and investigation. The staff attorney frequently will request additional information that he considers necessary for the determination of the claim. When he is satisfied that all sources of evidence and relevant information have been exhausted, he may recommend that the Commission do one of a number of things. First, the Commission, on its own initiative or upon the claimant's application for good cause shown, may direct that a conference be held with respect to any issue involved in the claim.[378] Second, it may order a hearing

---

[370] 64 Stat. 14 (1950), 22 U.S.C. § 1623(d) (1958). See also 45 C.F.R. § 501.5 (1960).

[371] 45 C.F.R. § 501.6 (1960).

[372] 45 C.F.R. § 531.3(a) (1960).

[373] *Ibid.*

[374] 45 C.F.R. § 531.3(b) (1960).

[375] *Ibid.*

[376] 45 C.F.R. § 531.3(c) (1960).

[377] 45 C.F.R. § 531.4 (1960).

[378] 45 C.F.R. § 531.7 (1960).

upon the claim, specifying the questions to which the hearing shall be limited.[379] Third, it may, without a conference or hearing, issue a proposed decision in determination of the claim.[380]

Little need be said about the informal presettlement conferences. They afford claimants' attorneys an opportunity to discuss the merits of their claims with the Commission's staff attorneys, and they permit the latter to point out possible weaknesses in a claim. It is at this stage of the claim that claimants most often are informed of evidence that the Commission has developed on its own initiative. Like pre-trial practice before federal courts, these conferences also serve the useful function of narrowing the issues and indicating the crucial questions on which the allowance or denial of a claim may turn. Finally, they provide an opportunity for the claimant to seek the Commission's help in acquiring evidence from abroad. In some cases the Commission has gone to great lengths to help claimants obtain needed evidence,[381] and not infrequently its cooperation has meant the difference between an award and a denial of a claim.[382]

If the Commission orders a hearing upon a claim or if a claimant, upon the issuance without a previous hearing of a proposed decision denying his claim in whole or in part, requests a hearing upon the claim,[383] a hearing will be held upon not less than fifteen

[379] 45 C.F.R. § 531.5(a) (1960).

[380] 45 C.F.R. § 531.5(b) (1960).

[381] See, *e.g.*, FCSC THIRTEENTH SEMIANN. REP. 4–5 (1960) (special representative stationed in Warsaw to obtain evidence concerning Polish claims).

[382] "It is fair to say in this regard that, if the Commission had not undertaken to obtain necessary evidence on behalf of claimants but had adhered strictly to the position that the burden of submitting all evidence was upon the claimant, at least 85% of all claims would have had to be denied." Clay, *Aspects of Settling Claims Under the Yugoslav Claims Agreement of 1948*, 43 GEO. L. J. 582, 592 (1955).

[383] In the case of a denial or partial denial of his claim, the claimant has a statutory right to a hearing. 64 Stat. 15–16 (1950), 22 U.S.C.

days' notice of the time and place thereof.[384] A hearing is conducted by the Commission in plenary session or by one or more of the three commissioners,[385] and it is open to the public unless otherwise requested by the claimant and ordered by the Commission.[386] The claimant, being the moving party, has the burden of proof on all issues involved in the determination of his claim.[387]

The conduct of a hearing has been described by a former chairman of the Foreign Claims Settlement Commission as follows:

> A hearing opens with a statement of the claim by the Commission attorney who has handled it, summarizing the evidence already before the Commission, pointing out its strengths and weaknesses, and stating the reason for the proposed decision. The claimant or his counsel then makes his opening statement followed by the production of any witnesses he may wish to call and the introduction of any other evidence he may wish to offer. . . . The witnesses may also be interrogated by members of the Commission's staff or by the Commissioners themselves or, more commonly, by both. The claimant's attorney

§ 1623(h) (1958). To secure a hearing the claimant must request the same within twenty days of the service of the proposed decision upon him or his attorney. 45 C.F.R. § 531.5(e) (1960). In addition to assigning the errors relied upon, the claimant should specify whether the hearing is for the taking of evidence or only for the presentation of oral argument. *Ibid.* If the claimant does not file objections or request a hearing within the twenty-day period (sixty days for Polish claims), the proposed decision automatically becomes the Commission's final determination and decision on the claim. 45 C.F.R. § 531.5(g) (Supp. 1962).

[384] 45 C.F.R. § 531.6(a) (1960).

[385] 45 C.F.R. § 531.6(c) (1960). See also Gillilland, *supra* note 366, at 17.

[386] 45 C.F.R. § 531.6(b) (1960).

[387] 45 C.F.R. § 531.6(d) (1960). See also FCSC 1959 REP. 104. Compare text note 382 *supra.*

then makes his oral argument. The Commission's attorney is not permitted to respond in argument in that we relentlessly require that members of our staff do their utmost to themselves maintain an objective and judicial attitude. Controversy is under no circumstances permitted. However, the Commission attorneys are permitted to interrogate claimants' attorneys at the hearings to bring out and give opportunity to explain what might be considered weaknesses in their positions.[388]

A hearing, then, is similar to a proceeding in an equity court, with the claimant permitted to appear, call witnesses, submit evidence, including depositions, and cross-examine Commission witnesses in those rare instances where they are used.[389] Commission personnel, however, have been enjoined to keep "procedures as non-adversary as it can and to prevent, at all levels of processing, either the appearance or the fact of 'opposition' to claims." [390] Attorneys for claimants, to quote a former chairman of the Commission once again,

> will find no opposing counsel, no opposing witnesses, no opposing briefs or arguments although his own witnesses may be

[388] *Hearing Before the Subcommittee on Commerce and Finance of the House Committee on Interstate and Foreign Commerce,* 86th Cong., 1st Sess. 11–12 (1959) (mimeographed statement of Hon. Whitney Gillilland). See also Gillilland, *supra* note 366, at 17–18.

[389] 45 C.F.R. § 531.6(c) (1960).

[390] Gillilland, *supra* note 366, at 17. Nevertheless, a Commission attorney has attested that he and his colleagues serve "as adversaries to the claimants in all hearings before the Commission. . . ." Rode, *The International Claims Commission of the United States,* 47 AM. J. INT'L L. 615, 621 (1953). It appears that Congress, when it enacted the legislation establishing the Commission, wanted the claims to be handled on an adversary basis. 95 CONG. REC. 8842 (1949) (Mr. Ribicoff). On the wisdom of this attitude, see LILLICH 51–53. See also Re, *The Foreign Claims Settlement Commission and International Claims,* 13 SYRACUSE L. REV. 516, 523 (1962).

cross-examined by the commissioners or members of the staff. On the other hand it is hoped that he can rely upon it that the Commission is not in any degree opposing his claim, but is only trying to become informed as to the facts and the law in order that its decision may go to the right of the matter.[391]

The foreign country involved may play an important role in allowing or denying awards if it agrees to cooperate with the Commission in the adjudicative process. Yugoslavia, for instance, had the right to file briefs amicus curiae before the Commission,[392] and it submitted evidence which resulted in the denial of claims.[393] Poland, by Article V of the 1960 claims agreement, indicated its willingness to furnish to the Commission all documents in its possession necessary to a just determination of claims.[394] Upon occasion, when the claimant has been unable to obtain documents fully substantiating his allegations as to ownership and extent of loss, the Commission nevertheless has rendered awards of less than the full amount claimed.[395]

After the conclusion of a hearing, upon the expiration of any time allowed by the Commission for further submissions, the Commission may proceed to a final decision and determination of the claim.[396] The final decision may affirm, reverse, or modify the

[391] Gillilland, *supra* note 366, at 18.

[392] Agreement With Yugoslavia, July 19, 1948, 62 Stat. 2662, T.I.A.S. No. 1803.

[393] Rode, *supra* note 389, at 634.

[394] Agreement With Poland, July 16, 1960 [1960] 11 U.S.T. & O.I.A. 1953, T.I.A.S. No. 4545. The procedure for obtaining evidence under Article V is spelled out in a Protocol With Poland, Nov. 29, 1960 [1960] 11 U.S.T. & O.I.A. 2450, T.I.A.S. No. 4629.

[395] See text at and accompanying note 283 *supra*.

[396] 45 C.F.R. § 531.5(i) (1960). A claimant may object to a proposed decision but not request a hearing, in which case the Commission will examine the entire record before reaching a final decision or ordering further proceedings. 45 C.F.R. § 531.5(h) (1960). In most cases a dis-

proposed decision.[397] Most hearings result in a decision of affirmance.[398] After a final decision has been issued on a claim, or a proposed decision has become the final decision of the Commission, a claimant may petition to reopen the claim on the ground of newly discovered evidence.[399] If the final decision is not reopened, the Commission's statute makes it "a full and final disposition of the case in which the decision is rendered." [400] The Commission thereupon certifies the award to the Secretary of the Treasury,[401] who is authorized and directed to pay to the awardee an amount not exceeding the principal of the certified award, plus accrued interest on such awards as bear interest.[402] Where the fund is not sufficient to pay all of the awards, awards of $1,000 or less are paid in full and larger ones are paid on a pro rata basis.[403] A sum representing five per cent of the claims fund is deducted from the fund to cover the Commission's operating costs.[404] Payments from lump sum settlements may be stretched out over a period of twenty years.[405]

Although no court in the United States has ever reviewed the decision of a national claims commission as to the validity of the claim or the amount of an award,[406] disappointed claimants con-

appointed claimant will demand a hearing, however, and the decisional process outlined in the text will be followed.

[397] 64 Stat. 16 (1950), 22 U.S.C. § 1623(h) (1958).

[398] See LILLICH 50, n. 178.

[399] 45 C.F.R. § 531.5(l) (1960). See Re, *supra* note 390, at 524.

[400] 64 Stat. 14 (1950), 22 U.S.C. § 1623(b) (1958).

[401] 64 Stat. 16 (1950), 22 U.S.C. § 1624 (1958).

[402] 64 Stat. 16 (1950), 22 U.S.C. § 1625 (1958).

[403] 64 Stat. 18 (1950), 22 U.S.C. § 1627 (1958).

[404] 67 Stat. 506 (1953), 22 U.S.C. § 1626(b) (1958).

[405] See Article I(B) of the Agreement With Poland, July 16, 1960 [1960] 11 U.S.T. & O.I.A. 1953, T.I.A.S. No. 4545.

[406] Courts have taken jurisdiction to determine title to awards. See, *e.g.*, Comegys v. Vasse, 26 U.S. (1 Pet.) 193 (1828); Frevall v. Bache, 39 U.S. (14 Pet.) 95 (1840); Judson v. Corcoran, 58 U.S. (17 How.) 612 (1854).

tinue to seek judicial review of Commission decisions.[407] Since the Supreme Court has held that a claims fund is a national fund to be distributed as Congress sees fit,[408] the executive department has taken the position that claimants have no right of judicial review absent clear congressional intent to the contrary.[409] Far from providing for such review, Congress has attempted to preclude it.[410] Thus the Foreign Claims Settlement Commission's enabling act specifically provides that:

> The action by the Commission in allowing or denying any claim under this Act shall be final and conclusive on all questions of law and fact and not subject to review by the Secretary of State or any other official, department, agency, or establishment of the United States or by any court by mandamus or otherwise.[411]

See, generally, Coerper, *The Foreign Claims Settlement Commission and Judicial Review*, 50 AM. J. INT'L L. 868 (1956).

[407] See, generally, LILLICH 58–70.

[408] Williams v. Heard, 140 U.S. 529 (1891).

[409] See, *e.g.*, De Vegvar v. Gillilland, 228 F.2d 640, 642 (D.C. Cir. 1955), *cert. denied*, 350 U.S. 994 (1956). Compare RESTATEMENT, FOREIGN RELATIONS, Explanatory Notes § 219, comment *a* at 730–31 (Proposed Official Draft, 1962).

[410] See LILLICH 55–58.

[411] 64 Stat. 16 (1950), 22 U.S.C. § 1623(h) (1958). This finality clause applies only to distributions from lump sum settlements. A 1955 statute under which the Commission made certain awards from vested assets and other funds contained a similar no-review provision. 69 Stat. 574 (1955), 22 U.S.C. § 1641(m) (1958). The 1958 act providing for the payment of Czech claims from vested assets did not have such a provision. *Quaere:* since the 1955 statute specifically excluded the possibility of review, could it not have been argued that the omission of a no-review provision in the Czech act indicated a Congressional intent to permit judicial review? But see the cases cited in note 406 *supra*, where judicial review of the amount and validity of national claims commission awards was denied despite the absence of finality provisions. See also Z. & F. Assets Corp. v. Hull, 311 U.S. 470 (1941).

Nevertheless, four recent decisions of the United States Court of Appeals for the District of Columbia, although all denying review, have delimited an area where Commission decisions might be reviewable. In *De Vegvar v. Gillilland*,[412] the court, brushing aside the above statute, stated:

> We may assume for purposes of argument that the provisions of Section 4(h) would probably not prevent judicial relief in the situation—to illustrate—where a claimant is denied consideration by reason of his race, creed or color. No violation of constitutional right is suggested here. . . .[413]

Thus the court, although it affirmed the complaint's dismissal, clearly implied that judicial intervention was proper to protect constitutional rights. Similar statements appear in *Haas v. Humphrey* [414] and *American and European Agencies v. Gillilland*.[415]

The most recent case raising the judicial review question, *First National City Bank of New York v. Gillilland*,[416] again saw the court finding no constitutional problem and refusing review. Citing the above three cases, the court pointedly noted that "these cases interpreting the nonreviewability clause of the International Claims Settlement Act say courts could intervene when constitutional rights have been violated, but none of these cases involved such a situation." [417] While it seems doubtful that the Foreign Claims Settlement Commission would ever commit error sufficient to constitute a violation of a claimant's constitutional rights, the possibility exists that judicial review might be

[412] 228 F.2d 640 (D.C. Cir. 1955), *cert. denied*, 350 U.S. 994 (1956).
[413] 228 F.2d at 642. See also Dayton v. Gillilland, 242 F.2d 227, 228 (D.C. Cir. 1957).
[414] 246 F.2d 682, 683 (D.C. Cir.), *cert. denied*, 355 U.S. 854 (1957).
[415] 247 F.2d 95, 97–98 (D.C. Cir.), *cert. denied*, 355 U.S. 884 (1957).
[416] 257 F.2d 223 (D.C. Cir.), *cert. denied*, 358 U.S. 837 (1958).
[417] 257 F.2d at 226, n. 1.

available in an appropriate case, at least in the District of Columbia Circuit.[418] As long as the Commission accords claimants procedural due process, however, its final decisions certainly will be held to be nonreviewable.[419]

INTERNATIONAL COMMISSIONS

In the past, whenever a large number of claims arose against a single foreign country, the United States attempted to negotiate an agreement with that country, submitting the claims to an international arbitral tribunal, usually a mixed claims commission, for adjudication.[420] The tribunal, usually composed of nationals of the United States, the foreign country, and a third state, would determine the validity of claims brought by the United States on behalf of its nationals against the foreign country. Although the Department of State professes some interest in this method of settling claims today,[421] the United States–Japanese Property Commission [422] and the United States–Italian Conciliation Commission [423] are the only instances of the utilization of this device by the United States since World War II.

Since it is apparent that most United States nationals with international claims against foreign countries will be presenting them, at least in the foreseeable future, to the Foreign Claims

[418] The Court of Appeals for the Sixth Circuit has stated categorically that "this is not an area where Constitutional limitations would prevent Congress from foreclosing judicial review." Zutich v. Gillilland, 254 F.2d 464, 465 (6th Cir. 1958).

[419] RESTATEMENT, FOREIGN RELATIONS, Explanatory Notes § 219, comment *a* at 730–31 (Proposed Official Draft, 1962). See Re, *supra* note 390, at 525.

[420] See, generally, LILLICH 6–15.

[421] See text at note 315 *supra*.

[422] See note 14 *supra*.

[423] See note 15 *supra*.

Settlement Commission,[424] no attempt will be made here to discuss the operations of international commissions. Ample literature exists about these commissions,[425] and in any event it would be of limited value to generalize about them since their operations are governed by the terms of the particular *compromis* and the rules of procedure adopted by the commission.[426] Should such commissions be used in the future, their operations would of necessity follow the submission of claims to the Department of State for espousal or negotiation purposes. The Department would notify claimants of the commission's existence and their rights to present a claim to it. The claimant would then prepare a statement of claim, similar in fashion to the one previously filed with the Department, which would be presented to the commission by an agent of the United States as its claim. The role of the claimant in the presentation of a claim to an international commission, then, is far less important than it is when the claimant appears before the Department of State or the Foreign Claims Settlement Commission.

[424] The Commission's enabling act contains a provision envisaging the administration of future claims programs. 64 Stat. 13–14 (1950), 22 U.S.C. §§ 1622(c), 1623(a) (1958). See, generally, LILLICH 9–10, 102–03. See also RESTATEMENT, FOREIGN RELATIONS, Explanatory Notes § 219, Reporter's Note at 731–32 (Proposed Official Draft, 1962).

[425] See, for example, SIMPSON & FOX, note 43 *supra;* CARLSTON, THE PROCESS OF INTERNATIONAL ARBITRATION (1946); HUDSON, INTERNATIONAL TRIBUNALS (1944); SANDIFER, note 139 *supra;* and RALSTON, THE LAW AND PROCEDURE OF INTERNATIONAL TRIBUNALS (1926, Supp. 1936).

[426] The Rules of Procedure of the United States–Japanese Property Commission may be found in Appendix F. See also Summers & Fraleigh, *The United States–Japanese Property Commission,* 56 AM. J. INT'L L. 407 (1962).

Appendixes

APPENDIX A

SAMPLE STATEMENT OF CLAIM IN AFFIDAVIT FORM [1]

Statement of Claim

I, Robert Thompson, being first duly sworn, depose and say:

1. I am an American citizen by virtue of naturalization before the District Court of the United States for the Southern District of the State of New York on September 15, 1935. In proof of that fact I attach hereto, as exhibit 1-A,[2] a copy of a letter to the Immigration and Naturalization

---

[1] This sample form for a taking of property claim is entirely hypothetical and should be used only as a guide in preparing a claim for presentation to the Department of State or to a national or international claims commission not having issued claims forms.

[2] The *figure 1* has reference to the related *paragraph of the affidavit* and the *letter A* to the first exhibit filed in support of that paragraph. Exhibits are not included with this form.

Service, Department of Justice, requesting that it send evidence of my naturalization to the Department of State, Washington 25, D.C. I was born at Liverpool, England, on August 16, 1900, came to the United States at the age of twenty (1920), and now have my permanent residence at San Diego, California. I have been a ranch owner and operator during the past forty years and, in addition to owning a large ranch in California, I also own a ranch and sugar plantation in Oriente Province, Cuba, where I have spent about half of my time during the past ten years. During that time I have made frequent visits to the United States. I have registered each year with the American Consul at Havana. That fact is verified by the Consul's letter of October 25, 1958, which is attached hereto as exhibit 1-B. Since 1960 I have remained in the United States because the present situation in Cuba precludes my return.

2. I am the owner of a tract of 3,000 hectares (7,413 acres) located in the Oriente Province, described in the Register of Titles No. 776 of the City of Juan. This land is about thirty kilometers from the City of Juan, near the Garcia branch of the Cuban National Railways, and was acquired by my father, Mr. Samuel Thompson, on January 18, 1930, by contract of purchase-sale with Joaquin Ramirez. My father died on April 11, 1932, leaving a will by which I was made his sole heir. That will was duly probated in the First District Court of First Instance of the City of Juan on July 6, 1932, and appropriately recorded in the office of Registrar of Titles on July 8, 1932.

I attach hereto in proof of the foregoing statements, and marked 2-A, 2-B, 2-C, and 2-D, respectively, the following documents:

2-A. A certified copy of the purchase-sale contract of January 18, 1930.

2-B. A certified photostat copy of my father's will of July 19, 1928.

2-C. A certified copy of the record of the First District Court of First Instance of the City of Juan, admitting my father's will to probate.

2-D. A certified copy of the registration of the probated will in the office of the Registrar of Titles.

3. The price paid by my father for the above-described property was fifty pesados (then twenty-five U.S. dollars at the rate of exchange then most favorable; Exhibit 3-A) per hectare or a total of one hundred and fifty thousand pesados. Of that amount, one hundred thousand pesados was paid in cash, and the balance was represented by a mortgage (hipoteca) which was liquidated and paid on September 17, 1931. The facts of (a) purchase price and (b) amount of the original mortgage are shown by the original contract of purchase-sale (Exhibit 2-A herewith). The fact of final payment of the original mortgage is shown by the certified copy of the record of cancellation thereof, as it appears in the office of the Registrar of Titles, which copy is attached hereto, marked Exhibit 3-B.

4. At the time of original purchase of the property by my father, it was in an almost completely unimproved condition, having at that time but fifty hectares under cultivation and buildings of very poor construction, worth, at the most, two thousand pesados. Those improvements have long since been replaced by modern buildings and other improvements have been added consisting of the following:

    a. A farm house, costing approximately $5,000.

    b. Six houses for servants and workmen, costing approximately $6,000.

    c. A barn, costing $3,500.

    d. A sugar processing plant, costing $45,000.

    e. A well, 150 feet deep, with windmill, costing $1,350.

    f. Fences costing approximately $2,750.

The total cost of the above-mentioned permanent improvements, which were made during the years 1930–1932, was $63,600.

While it is impossible to state, specifically, the amount spent annually in the form of upkeep of such permanent improvements, I declare, on my oath, that the amount has not been less, and is actually more, than their original cost.

In proof of the foregoing statements I attach to this affidavit the following documents:

    a. An affidavit of Ralph R. Jones, the contractor-builder who was in charge of the construction of the above-mentioned houses and barn. These buildings were erected on a basis of cost plus 12 per cent and both he and I well remember that this total commission amounted to $1,750. Jones' affidavit is marked 4-A.

    b. An affidavit of Lucius Fenwig, who was foreman for Jones in the erection of the buildings and who is also entirely familiar with the cost thereof. His affidavit is marked 4-B.

    c. A certified copy of the contract of March 16, 1930 with engineer Michael Bates, in pursuance of which the sugar processing plant was built and the well drilled. This contract is marked 4-C.

    d. The original invoice for the windmill, and the freight invoice showing original cost and transportation cost thereof to have been $750 and $87.50, respectively. These documents are marked 4-D and 4-E, respectively. I have not included in the cost of the windmill the cost of erection since that was done by Mr. Bates without charge.

    e. The affidavits of Garcia Romero and Juan Cortez, respectively, Manager and Assistant Manager of my hacienda, who were in charge of the building of the fences thereon and who are thoroughly familiar with the original cost thereof and with their present condition, as shown by their affidavits, which are marked 4-F and 4-G, respectively. I also attach the sworn statement of Miguel Cabeza, formerly mayor of the City of Juan, who is himself a ranch and plantation owner, who is thoroughly familiar with values in the vicinity of my ranch and plantation and who volunteered to inspect the above-mentioned improvements and to certify to the valuation thereof. His affidavit which, in general, supports the above evidence on the question of valuation of the permanent improvements, is marked 4-H.

f. Six unmounted photographs of the permanent improvements which I attach hereto and which are marked 4-I, 4-J, 4-K, 4-L, 4-M, and 4-N.

5. At the time of the purchase of the farm by my father, it was in a practically abandoned condition having been left in charge of a laborer. I am unable to state definitely whether or not the purchase price included any personal property. However, the movable property on the land at the time of purchase consisted of a few dilapidated farm tools and about ten head of cattle and mules, worth a maximum of 2,000 pesados which, without knowing that they were included in the purchase price, I am willing to concede were so included, reducing the net cost of the land to 148,000 pesados. I submit as corroborating proof of the state of the ranch at the time of purchase the affidavit of the seller, Joaquin Ramirez, which is marked 5-A.

At the time of the seizure of my property by the Cuban authorities, there were on the estate the following personal properties:

a. Farm implements to the value of $3,500.
b. Tools, et cetera to the value of $300.
c. 25 mules of the average value of $50, or a total of $1,250.
d. 500 head of cattle of an average value of $30, or a total of $15,000.
e. 200 acres of cane of an average value, for the mature but un-harvested crop, of $35 per acre, or a total of $7,000.
f. Furniture in seven houses, to the value of $3,750.

These facts are proven by the above-mentioned affidavit of Miguel Cabeza (Exhibit 4-H herewith), by five photographs of the growing crops which I attach and mark 5-B, 5-C, 5-D, 5-E, and 5-F, respectively, and by the joint affidavit of Horace Winters and Juan Perez, former agricultural experts of the Cuban Government, testifying to the value of unharvested crops of equal quality at the date of seizure. That joint affidavit is marked 5-G.

6. The lands belonging to me which were expropriated by the Cuban authorities under the agrarian laws include about 300 hectares (741 acres). The expropriations were effected by two proceedings, one initiated before the Local Agrarian Commission on November 3, 1959, which terminated with the Ministerial Decree No. 873 of June 10, 1960,

the other by proceedings which were begun on April 10, 1960, and terminated with the Ministerial Decree No. 1472 of August 11, 1960. The first of these expropriations comprised approximately 145 hectares, and the second one about 155 hectares.

There are attached herewith as proof of the expropriations photostat copies of the two above-mentioned Ministerial Decrees as they appeared in the Official Gazette of the Republic of Cuba under dates of June 18, 1960, and August 16, 1960, respectively. Those exhibits are marked 6-A and 6-B.

These expropriations were allegedly made for purposes of economic reform, and although I did everything possible, through appeals to the Local Agrarian Commission, the National Agrarian Reform Institute, and the Minister of Finance, to protect my interests and to preserve my estate, my petitions were disregarded and the expropriations, as originally petitioned for, were finally carried out, no compensation having been paid to me.

7. Along with the land expropriated, the Cuban authorities took all of the personal property belonging to the estate with the exception of 400 head of cattle left on the grazing lands not expropriated. Such property is listed, in general terms, in paragraph 5 above and, omitting the cattle not seized, is valued at $15,050. A detailed, sworn inventory of the property taken is attached hereto marked 7-A.

8. I estimate the amount to which I am entitled, on account of the expropriation of my land and permanent improvements thereon, as follows:

a. Value of 300 hectares of highly improved agricultural land at $100 per hectare .... $ 30,000.
b. Value of the permanent improvements thereon, including a sugar processing plant, as shown in paragraph 4 above, less $2,000 representing the value of fences on unseized lands .... $ 61,600.
c. Reduction of value of the unseized lands, 2,700 hectares, at $20 per hectare .... $ 54,000.

Total .... $145,600.

In support of item (c) above I declare that my estate had its maximum value as a complete operating unit, each portion of which complemented the rest, and that the expropriation of the highly developed portion reduced the value of the remaining lands which are used for growing cane and for grazing purposes. Therefore, whereas the unseized portion of the estate, as a part of the estate, had a value of approximately $108,000 (or $40 per hectare), cut off from the improved portions of the property it is worth, as a maximum, $20 per hectare. In corroboration of that statement, I submit the affidavits of Juan Babtista, Enrique Suarez and Henry Thomason, each of whom formerly owned land in the vicinity of the seized property at the time of the expropriations and is therefore fully competent to testify as an expert witness regarding the value of that property and other facts. Their affidavits are marked 8-A, 8-B and 8-C. In further support of items (a), (b) and (c) I submit the sworn statement of Robert Grimes, registered engineer, who is qualified to calculate the value at the time of seizure and the consequent reduction of value in the land not seized (Exhibit 8-D).

9. The total value of the personal property seized is $15,050. Proof of that fact is contained in the attached inventory marked 7-A, together with the affidavit of my accountant James Harrison (which is marked 9-A) which I ask to have considered jointly with exhibits 4-H, 5-B, 5-C, 5-D, 5-E, 5-F, and 5-G.

10. My whole estate was under mortgage, in the amount of $75,000 (originally $100,000) to Gonzales Amador, a Cuban national. A copy of that mortgage is attached hereto marked 10-A. There is also attached a certificate showing that Mr. Amador is a Cuban national (marked 10-B) and a letter from Mr. Amador (marked 10-C) in which he admits that the unpaid balance is now $75,000.

11. The amounts paid as taxes on my estate in 1958, before the above-mentioned expropriation, were as follows:

Land tax ....$2,000.
Personal property tax ....$ 150.
Total ....$2,150.

There are attached hereto as proof of those facts the paid tax bills, dated June 30, 1958 and September 10, 1958, which are marked 11-A and 11-B, respectively.

12. I declare that I have neither received nor been offered anything whatever of value in exchange for the lands expropriated.

13. During the pendency of the expropriation proceedings I expended in an effort to defend my rights the sum of $3,600, made up as follows:

Attorney's fees ....$2,500.
Court costs ....   200.
Miscellaneous ....   900.
Total ....$3,600.

These expenses are fully detailed in the attached affidavit of my attorney (Pascual Syndico) to which is attached all available paid bills. That affidavit is marked Exhibit 13-A.

14. At the time of the expropriation proceedings (referred to in

paragraph 6 above) the Local Agrarian Commission seized in all 450 hectares, 150 of which were subsequently returned to me. The Local Agrarian Commission which made the original seizure of this 150 hectares was composed of Juan Arosamina, Emilio Sanchez, Fernando Rodriguez, Tomas Tomasillo and Guillermo Casis, all of whom are residents of the City of Juan. The order of seizure was dated December 6, 1959. Appeal from this order was taken to the National Agrarian Reform Institute which approved the seizure on July 8, 1960. From that decision an appeal was taken to the Ministry of Finance which ordered the return of the 150 acres on December 15, 1960.

The property so seized consisted of forested lands, adjoining my improved estate. Its value at the time of seizure was forty dollars per hectare, principally because of the timber thereon. While in the custody of agents of the Local Agrarian Commission, at least 50 per cent of my standing timber was cut and either utilized or destroyed. The damage done in that connection was therefore at least $2,500, not counting the cost of clearing away the waste timber left by the temporary occupants. The cost of defending my interests before the Local Agrarian Commission, the National Agrarian Reform Institute and the Ministry of Finance in connection with that seizure was $784. I therefore suffered damage in that connection in the amount of $3,284.

In proof of the foregoing, I attach hereto the following:

(14-A) A certified copy of the decision of the Ministry of Finance ordering the return of the 150 hectares in question.

(14-B) A paid, itemized account of my attorney, Josef Leastro, showing his fees, court costs, stamp charges, and miscellaneous expenses.

(14-C) A joint affidavit of William Warren, Harold Clay and Josiah Boyce, testifying to the value of the land before seizure, the nature of the damages done and the value of the land at present.

(14-D and 14-E) Photographs of the property before and after seizure.

15. There is now in custody of the so-called agrarians a further quantity of 120 hectares which they were put in possession of by the above-mentioned Local Agrarian Commission on April 27, 1960. I have an appeal pending before the Ministry of Finance against that seizure but I do not expect a favorable decision. I therefore include in this claim the amount of $1,000 representing the value of the loss of possession and use of the 120 hectares in question.

In proof of the foregoing statements I attach hereto a certified copy of the order of the Local Agrarian Commission, dated April 27, 1960

(Exhibit 15-A), and also a certified copy of my appeal to the Ministry of Finance (Exhibit 15-B). I also refer, in that connection, to the exhibits listed in paragraphs 6, 8 and 14.

In summary my claim totals $168,534, which amount is made up as follows:

a. Land expropriated (paragraph 8) ....$ 30,000.
b. Permanent improvements and sugar processing plant (paragraph 8) .... 61,600.
c. Reduction of value of unexpropriated land (paragraph 8) 54,000.
d. Personal property (paragraph 9) .... 15,050.
e. Expenses (paragraph 13) .... 3,600.
f. Temporary seizure, including expenses, (paragraph 14) .. 3,284.
g. Loss of possession and use flowing from incomplete seizure (paragraph 15) .... 1,000.

Total ....$168,534.

Signed ROBERT THOMPSON

Personally appeared before me, J. Piercy Fragner, a Notary Public in and for the State of California, this 30th day of November 1961, Robert Thompson, the person who signed the foregoing affidavit in my presence, who, being personally known to me, after being duly sworn has deposed and said that he has carefully read all of the preceding affidavit and that the same is in every respect true and correct to his own personal knowledge.

(Signed) J. PIERCY FRAGNER
Notary Public

(Notarial Seal)
My Commission expires January 10, 1963.

APPENDIX B

FCSC Form 709

Budget Bureau No. 91–6001.

FOREIGN CLAIMS SETTLEMENT COMMISSION
OF THE UNITED STATES
Washington 25, D.C.

IN THE MATTER OF THE CLAIM OF

CLAIM NO. PO...

Under the Polish Claims Agreement of 1960 and Title I of the International Claims Settlement Act of 1949, as amended.

DO NOT WRITE IN THIS SPACE

An original and *two* copies of this form and each supporting exhibit must be filed. Each document in a foreign language must be accompanied by a verified English translation. Answers should be typed or printed. Attach additional sheets as needed for any items where space on the form is insufficient. The information and instruction sheet attached hereto with directions for each numbered item on the claim form was prepared for the purpose of assisting you in the preparation of your claim. It is suggested that you read it thoroughly before completing this claim form. Time for filing expires at midnight, 12:00 p.m., September 30, 1961.

1. Name of claimant ....
   (Last)   (First)   (Middle)

2. Address of claimant ....

3. Name and address of attorney (if any) ....

SUMMARY OF LOSSES CLAIMED

	Where located	Amount in dollars	Total claimed
4. Real estate:			
(a) Land		$.............	
(b) Buildings		....	$.............
5. Personal property, furniture, equipment, merchandise, etc.	. . . .	....	
6. Stock shares (name of corporation	....)	....	
7. Debts:			
(a) Owed by nationalized enterprises	. . . .	$.............	
(b) Charges upon property nationalized or taken	. . . .	....	$.............
8. TOTAL AMOUNT CLAIMED	. . . .	. . . .	$.............

9. If claimant is an individual, indicate how nationality was acquired (check one), and submit supporting documentary evidence.

   ☐ Birth . . . . . Date .... Place ....
   ☐ Naturalization . . Date .... Place .... Cert. No. ....
   ☐ Marriage . . . . Date .... Name of spouse ....
   ☐ Through parents . Date .... Name of parent(s) ....

DO NOT DETACH.—THIS ACKNOWLEDGMENT WILL BE RETURNED WITH THE CLAIM NUMBER

Fill in below the name and address of the person to whom receipt is to be sent.

CLAIM RECEIPT

This will acknowledge receipt of claim, NUMBERED PO..................... under the Polish Claims Agreement of 1960. In all correspondence with the Foreign Claims Settlement Commission please refer to this number.

CLAIMANT'S name if different from addressee:

....

NAME ....

ADDRESS ....

CITY AND STATE ....

DO NOT WRITE IN THIS SPACE

DATE RECEIVED

U.S. GOVERNMENT PRINTING OFFICE : 1960—O—559421

125

INTERNATIONAL CLAIMS

Correspondence Concerning Claims.—The Commission will acknowledge receipt of each claim, and notify the claimant or his attorney of the claim number assigned to it, which number should be used on all further correspondence and papers filed concerning the claim.

Payment of Awards.—After a determination is made by the Foreign Claims Settlement Commission that the claimant is entitled to an award, such award is certified to the Secretary of the Treasury for payment. Payments are to be made in full of the principal of each award of $1,000 or less from the Polish Claims Fund. On any award the principal amount of which exceeds $1,000, only $1,000 will be paid initially. After such payments are made, payments will be made on the unpaid principal in ratable proportions. No payment of interest will be made until principal amounts of all awards have been paid in full.

Clerk of the Commission.

10. Has evidence of claimant's United States nationality ever been filed with the Foreign Claims Settlement Commission? .... (Yes or no). If answer is yes, identify claim in which such evidence was filed ....

11. Has claimant ever lost his United States nationality? .... (Yes or no). If yes, attach a statement of the circumstances, reasons, and present status.

12. If claimant is a corporation or other juridical person, attach a statement regarding ownership and qualifications in accordance with the conditions of eligibility set out in the Agreement Annex. Has the corporation or other juridical person been reorganized through judicial proceedings after the property was nationalized or taken by Poland? .... (Yes or no).

13. Detailed description of the property, rights and interests upon which claim is based. (Nature, location, street, number, city, county, lot number, area, etc., itemize personalty. Show the value of each item at the time of loss.)

    ....

    ....

    ....

    ....

    ....

    ....

    ....

14. When and how property was acquired:

    (a) If purchased, when .... consideration paid ....

    (b) If inherited, when .... from whom ....

    ...., Value at time inherited (in zlotys) ....

    What was nationality of the previous owner? ....

    (c) If acquired by inheritance was claimant's title officially recorded by a court? .... (Yes or no). If yes, identify court and give date, attaching the decree as an exhibit. If no, on a separate sheet give a family tree or outline showing from whom and when you acquired your interest.

    (d) Cost of improvements (not repairs), if any, made since acquisition ....

15. Was the property damaged during the war? .... (Yes or no). If yes, to what extent had the damage been repaired at the date of deprivation and at whose expense? (War damage is not compensable under the Agreement.) ....

....

....

16. (a) Date the claim arose (when property was nationalized, appropriated, or otherwise taken) ...., as a result of the following actions: (identify law, decree, or governmental action, if known) ....

....

....

(b) If property was not owned by claimant on the date it was taken, give name and nationality of the owner at that time, and all subsequent owners of the claim to the date of acquisition by claimant.

....	....
(Name)	(Nationality)
....	....
(Name)	(Nationality)

(c) Has any other person, firm, corporation, or legal entity now, or since the date of nationalization or other taking, had any interest in the property above described or in the claim hereby asserted? (If there is or has been any such other interest, indicate the names, present addresses, and nationality of all such interested parties.)

....

....

....

Attach as exhibits all documents pertaining to the foregoing.

17. (a) Has claimant filed or asserted any claim with respect to the subject matter of this claim or any related matter with or against any other agency of the United States Government or any foreign government? .... (Yes or no). If answer is yes, give date of filing, agency or foreign government with which claim was filed, amount claimed, disposition of claim, and amount of award, if any.

....

....

(b) Apart from this claim, has claimant or any predecessor in interest received, or has he any reason to expect to receive, any benefits, pecuniary or otherwise, on account of the loss resulting from the action for which this claim is filed? (If so, explain.)

....

....

(c) Has a tax deduction ever been asserted by claimant or any other predecessor in title of this claim with respect to losses described in this claim? .... (Yes or no). If answer is yes, give year such claim was asserted, amount of loss claimed, whether loss was allowed, amount allowed, and name of person claiming such a tax deduction.

....

....

127

INTERNATIONAL CLAIMS

18. Was the property reported to the United States Treasury Department on Form TFR–500, Census of Property in Foreign Countries (1943)? .... (Yes or no). If yes, what value was reported?

----

19. Set forth any additional facts pertinent to this claim. ....

IMPORTANT: ALL QUESTIONS CONTAINED ON THIS FORM MUST BE ANSWERED. If claimant does not know the answer to a question or the question is not applicable to his claim, claimant should write "UNKNOWN" or "INAPPLICABLE" in the proper space.

20. (In the case of an individual claimant.) The undersigned states that he is the claimant herein; that he has read the foregoing statement of claim and each statement and exhibit attached thereto and knows the contents thereof; that the same is true to his own knowledge, except as to matters therein stated to be alleged on information and belief, and that as to those matters he believes them to be true.

Dated ...., 196........   ....

(Signature or mark)

If by mark, two witnesses:

Name ....   Address ....

Name ....   Address ....

----

21. (For use in the case of a corporate or other entity claimant.) The undersigned states that he is the

.... of the claimant herein; that he is duly authorized to sign and
(Title or Office)
file this claim on behalf of the claimant; that he has read the foregoing statement of claim and each statement and exhibit attached thereto and knows the contents thereof; that the same is true to his own knowledge, except as to matters therein stated to be alleged on information and belief, and that as to those matters he believes them to be true.

Dated ...., 196..

(Signature)

SEAL (if any; if none, so state).

U.S. GOVERNMENT PRINTING OFFICE : 1960—O—559421

APPENDIXES

FOREIGN CLAIMS SETTLEMENT COMMISSION OF THE UNITED STATES

Washington 25, D.C.

INFORMATION AND INSTRUCTIONS FOR PREPARING AND FILING CLAIMS AGAINST POLAND UNDER THE·POLISH CLAIMS AGREEMENT OF 1960 AND TITLE I OF THE INTERNATIONAL CLAIMS SETTLEMENT ACT OF 1949, AS AMENDED.

General Statement

READ CAREFULLY BEFORE COMPLETING CLAIM FORM

Eligible Claims.—The Polish Claims Agreement signed July 16, 1960 provides for payment of $40,000,000 in full settlement and. discharge of all claims of *nationals of the United States,* whether natural or juridical persons, against the Government of Poland on account of the nationalization or other taking by Poland of property and rights and interests in and with respect to property, which occurred on or before the date of the Agreement.

Three classes of claims are included: claims of nationals of the United States for (*a*) the nationalization or other taking by Poland of property, and of rights and interests in and with respect to property; (*b*) the appropriation or the loss of use or enjoyment of property under Polish laws, decrees or other measures limiting or restricting rights and interests in and with respect to property; and (*c*) debts owed by enterprises which have been nationalized or taken by Poland and debts which were a charge upon property which has been nationalized, appropriated or otherwise taken by Poland.

"Claims of nationals of the United States," as used in the Agreement, means rights and interests in and with respect to property nationalized, appropriated or otherwise taken by Poland, *which from the date of such nationalization, appropriation or other taking to the date of the Agreement have been continuously owned by nationals of the United States.* (See the Agreement Annex for qualifications for juridical claimants and claims based upon indirect ownership through juridical persons.) *The property upon which the claim is based must have been owned by a person* (*or persons*) *who was a United States citizen on the date it was taken by the Polish Government.* (Roszczenia winne być własnością osób które od daty przejęcia przez Polskę mienia będącego podstawą roszczeń, do dnia 16-go lipca, t.j. do dnia podpisania układu były nieprzerwanie obywatelami Stanów Zjednoczonych.)

War damage claims, government bond claims (national, municipal, etc.), and claims based on taking by governments other than Poland are not covered by the Agreement.

Claim Filing Period.—Claims authorized under the Polish Claims Agreement must be filed with the Commission on or before September 30, 1961. If you are not able to support your claim completely by documentary evidence before the filing period expires, file the claim form and available evidence before September 30, 1961, and submit the additional evidence promptly when it is obtained.

.**Statement of Claim.**—Statements of claim must be prepared and filed in triplicate on FCSC Form 709, signed by claimants and delivered or forwarded by mail to the Foreign Claims Settlement Commission, Washington 25, D.C., not later than September 30, 1961. Statements of claim should include all items of loss incurred by claimants. Corporations or other entities should affix their corporate seal to each copy of their statements of claim.

Joint Claims.—If husband and wife, brothers and sisters, etc., have joint interests, it is preferable that they file a single claim.

Attorneys' Fees.—For limitations on attorney fees refer to Section 4(f) of the International Claims Settlement Act of 1949, as amended.

Exhibits and Documents in Support of Claim.—Originals of all exhibits and documents should be submitted with the claim, if available. If not available by the final date for filing, submit claim form before September 30, 1961, and file documents promptly thereafter when obtained. Verified translations into English must accompany all documents in a foreign language. The person making the translation shall sign a certificate similar to the following:

"I hereby certify that I am thoroughly familiar with the

.... language; that I have read the attached document written in said language; and that the attached English·translation thereof was made by me and is a true and accurate translation."

Signed ....

(Name)

....

(Address)

Previously Filed Claims.—You must file a claim on the attached form before September 30, 1961, even if you have filed other papers, forms, or documents with this Commission or any other agency or government with respect to your losses in Poland. Previous registration of your claim with the Commission is NOT a filing under the Polish Claims Agreement of 1960.

Penalty.—Any claimant, or any person filing any claim on behalf of a claimant, who knowingly and willfully conceals a material fact or makes a false statement or representation with respect to any matter before the Commission shall, under law, forfeit all rights to any award or·payment on account of this claim and in addition shall be subject to the criminal penalties provided in Title 18, United States Code, Section 1001.

All statements by persons other than the claimant which may be submitted in support of this claim shall include the following:

"The undersigned is aware that this·statement is to be submitted to the Foreign Claims Settlement Commission of the United States in connection with the claim of ..(Name of claimant) and that any willfully false statement herein may subject the undersigned to the criminal penalties provided by law in such cases."

IMPORTANT: ALL·QUESTIONS INCLUDED IN THE STATEMENT OF CLAIM FORM MUST BE ANSWERED. THE STATEMENT OF CLAIM MUST BE SIGNED.

DETACH THIS INSTRUCTION SHEET AND DO NOT RETURN WITH THE COMPLETED CLAIM FORM.

129

INTERNATIONAL CLAIMS

INSTRUCTIONS FOR COMPLETING FCSC FORM NO. 709

The items listed below are numbered to correspond to the items or questions on the application form.

Item No. 1.—If claimant is an individual, give name in full—last, first, middle—indicating any other names heretofore used; if claimant is a corporation or other legal entity, give the entity's full name, indicating any other names it has used. If claimant is other than an individual or corporation (e.g., partnership, association, trust, decedent's estate, minor's estate, etc.) state its character and attach a copy of the partnership agreement, articles of association, trust indenture, letters of administration or letters testamentary, together with certified copy of probated will, etc., whichever is appropriate. If the claimant is asserting a claim in a fiduciary capacity, describe the capacity of the claimant and the names, addresses, and the nature and extent of the interests of all beneficiaries, indicating the nationality of each such beneficiary on a separate sheet.

Item No. 2.—If claimant is an individual, give present residence; if claimant is a corporation, other legal entity, or partnership, etc., give principal place of business. Note.—It is important that the Commission be notified immediately of any change in claimant's address, or his status (i.e., death, marriage, etc.). The same holds true as to dissolution, reorganization, or other changes in the status of corporations or entities filing claims or having an interest in a claim.

Item No. 3.—A person may be represented by an attorney at law admitted to practice before any State of the United States or the District of Columbia, however, claimants are not required to be represented by an attorney.

Item No. 4.—Give the dollar amount claimed for (a) all unimproved land and (b) all improved real estate in the first column with the total amount claimed for these two categories in the column marked "Total claimed." Give Polish names for locations.

Item No. 5.—Give total dollar amount claimed for all personal property except stock shares, securities, and notes.

Item No. 6.—Give total dollar amount claimed for stock share interests in assets of nationalized corporations. Give names of nationalized corporations on a separate sheet if space is not sufficient.

Item No. 7.—Give dollar amount claimed for (a) debts of nationalized enterprises, and (b) mortgages, liens, and other charges upon property taken, in the first column with the total of the two in the column marked "Total claimed."

Item No. 8.—Show the total of items 4, 5, 6, and 7 as the total amount of the claim in dollars.

Item No. 9.—A native-born American citizen should submit a birth certificate or, if such certificate is not obtainable, a baptismal certificate, a certified copy of the record of baptism, passports, etc. A naturalized person, or a person who acquired United States citizenship by marriage or through his parent(s) must complete, in duplicate, and return to this Commission the enclosed "Request for Confirmation of Naturalization," Form DSP-13. Do NOT send this form to the Immigration and Naturalization Service.

Item No. 10.—If claimant has filed proof of United States nationality in a claim previously filed with the Foreign Claims Settlement Commission or its predecessors, it is not necessary to file further proof thereof *provided that there has been no change* in the nationality status of such claimant.

Item No. 11.—If the claimant has at any time lost his United States nationality, a detailed statement should be attached indicating when and how such nationality was lost, and when and how it was reacquired, together with all pertinent documentary evidence.

Item No. 12.—In case of claims by corporations or other legal entities, proof of 50 percent or more ownership by natural persons who were United States citizens will, wherever feasible, be established as indicated in Item 9 above.

Where stockholders are many in number, the Commission will consider a sworn statement by the secretary or other principal officer of the corporation (or other legal entity) certifying, for claims based upon direct ownership by juridical persons, as to the percentages of the outstanding capital stock or proprietary interest owned by nationals of the United States at the date of taking and continuously until the date of the Polish Claims Agreement.

Item No. 13.—Describe in detail the property involved and submit photographs, if available. Include a statement indicating the nature and extent of the claimant's interest therein. Give the location of the property at the time of its nationalization or other taking, with Polish names of the municipality and county, identify real property by land register, liber and lot number, street name and house number. Give exact area in local measurements. Itemize all articles of personalty. Explain how the value of the property at the time of loss, as given in Items 4 through 7, was computed. If any items entering into the computation of the loss, such as original purchase price, cost of improvements, etc., were expended in foreign currencies, indicate as to all such items, the amount in such currencies and the date of the expenditure. Attach all documents available to claimant evidencing the foregoing, including contracts of sale, all pertinent insurance and tax appraisals and valuations, mortgage or other lien encumbrances, etc.

Item No. 14.—In the event the property was inherited from a decedent who died intestate and no proceedings have been instituted in connection with his estate, give his Polish name in full, relationship to the claimant, and submit a certified copy of decedent's death certificate or, if none is available, other documentary proof on which you rely to establish his death and the date thereof. In such event submit, also, claimant's affidavit and the affidavits of two others who are familiar with the facts, reciting the names, ages, addresses, and nationality of all relatives surviving.

Item No. 15.—Losses due to war damage or claims based on taking by governments other than Poland are NOT compensable under the Polish Claims Agreement. However, information concerning war damage to the property and repairs made is important in determining value at the time the property was taken. Additionally, you may have a valid claim for war damage losses under future legislation. In the event compensation for certain war losses is provided by the Congress, the Commission will attempt to notify you so that a claim may be filed.

Item No. 16.—With respect to Question 16(a) the claimant should identify, if known, by number and date, the particular law or decree by which the property described in his claim was nationalized or taken by the Government of Poland and the date it was actually applied to the property. If this cannot be done at the time of filing, he should so state in his application and immediately attempt to ascertain the identity of such law or decree and inform the Commission accordingly. Reports, letters indicating status of the property, etc., should be submitted. (b) If the claimant was not the owner of the property at the time of nationalization or other taking, state the name and nationality of the owner at that time and all subsequent owners of the claim resulting from such taking to the date of acquisition by claimant.

Items Nos. 17, 18, 19.—No special instructions.

Items Nos. 20 and 21.—In addition to the penalties provided in Title 18, United States Code, Section 1001, any person guilty of any act, as provided therein, with respect to any matter under Title I of the International Claims Settlement Act of 1949, as amended, shall forfeit all rights under the title, and if payment shall have been made or granted, the Commission shall take such action as may be necessary to recover the same.

U.S. GOVERNMENT PRINTING OFFICE : 1960—O—559421

APPENDIX C

For Personal Injury or Loss of Life – July 1, 1955

First: Claim should be prepared in form of sworn statement, *in triplicate*. It should contain in narrative form a clear chronological statement of the essential facts relating to:

    a. American citizenship of the claimant. If the claim is based upon loss of life the American citizenship of both the claimant and the deceased must be established.

    b. The relationship of the claimant to the deceased in death cases.

    c. Time, place, and circumstances under which the injury or death occurred, including the identity of persons, officials, or agencies causing the injury or death.

    d. Nature and extent of damages sustained.

Second: Statements of claimants in support of claims, even when under oath, must be corroborated by other evidence. Accordingly, there should be attached to the sworn statement of claim, documentary evidence consisting of *original* documents or *certified copies* of originals, affidavits, etc., to support all material allegations in the sworn statement. The documents filed as evidence should be numbered consecutively and cited by number immediately after the allegations in the sworn statement in support of which the documents are filed.

All documents filed as evidence, as well as the affidavit of claimant, should be *in triplicate*.

Documents in other than the English language of which use is made, must be accompanied by authentic English translations.

Third: Nature of evidence required.

I. *Nationality.*

    1. If native-born:

Certified copy of birth certificate. If such certificate is unobtainable, and absence thereof is explained, claimant should furnish baptismal certificate or the affidavits of at least two persons (if affidavit of parent not obtainable) having personal knowledge of the facts, stating date and place of claimant's birth and basis of affiant's knowledge. Since citizenship of an American woman married prior to September 22, 1922 followed

131

that of her husband, proof of the latter's American citizenship must be furnished in such cases, together with a copy of the marriage certificate.

2. If naturalized:

Date and place of naturalization, designation of court and certificate number should be supplied.

Claimant should furnish same information to Immigration and Naturalization Service, Department of Justice, Washington 25, D.C., and request that Service to send to the Department of State a statement concerning such naturalization. Claimants having had communications from the Department of State with respect to their claims should also inform the Immigration and Naturalization Service of the Department's file number indicated on such correspondence, and request the Service to refer to such file number when furnishing this Department with information regarding the naturalization.

II. *Acts causing injury or death.*

1. Affidavits of eye-witnesses to the commission of the acts or of persons having personal and reliable knowledge of the circumstances surrounding the commission thereof, and identifying as far as possible the responsible persons, officials, or agencies.

2. Any other evidence tending to support claimant's allegations with reference to the cause of the injury or death, such, for example, as records of court proceedings or other public records.

III. *Proof of damages sustained.*

1. Injury cases.

The evidence filed in support of a claim based upon *personal injuries* should establish in as convincing manner as possible the following:

a. The age of the claimant and his earning capacity at the time of injury.

b. Extent of medical and hospital expenses occasioned by the injury.

c. Extent of injuries and physical suffering resulting therefrom.

d. Loss of time from gainful employment.

e. Extent of temporary or permanent impairment of earning capacity.

f. Amount of insurance or other indemnity, if any, collected or payable on account of the injury.

2. Death cases.

Claims based upon loss of life should be supported by evidence to establish the following:

a. Age of deceased and of the claimant and the earning capacity of each.

b. Relationship of claimant to the deceased.

    c. Extent of contributions made by the deceased toward support of claimant.

    d. Expenses incurred by claimant in connection with the death of the deceased, such as medical and hospital care, etc.

    e. Amount of insurance or other indemnity collected or payable by reason of death of the deceased.

The foregoing should not be understood to comprehend all essential requirements in the preparation of a claim. The suggestions are offered simply as a guide for that purpose. Variation in the facts of particular cases may require special treatment and methods of proof. For example, claims based upon alleged mistreatment of American nationals while in the custody of authorities of a foreign government, should, of course, disclose clearly the nature of the treatment complained of, the place or places where it occurred and the duration of the period over which the mistreatment was suffered. All material allegations of a claimant must be supported by convincing evidence; otherwise, the claim may be disallowed for lack of proof.

So far as concerns the amount of damages or losses claimed, it should be observed that the making of claims in exaggerated amounts, which cannot be substantiated by satisfactory evidence or otherwise justified, usually has a prejudicial effect and should, therefore, be avoided.

A careful observance of these suggestions in preparing claims will facilitate, to a great extent, consideration of the claims by such agency as may be entrusted with that responsibility. It should be clearly understood that the responsibility for preparing their claims and obtaining appropriate evidence in support of allegations rests entirely with the claimants.

In cases in which claimants are represented by an attorney, the latter should file a power of attorney evidencing his authority to act in such capacity.

APPENDIX D

For Loss of or Damage to Real or Personal Property – March 1, 1961

First: Claim should be prepared in form of sworn statement, *in triplicate*. It should contain in narrative form a clear chronological statement of the essential facts relating to:
  a. Citizenship of claimant or claimants.
  b. Full description of the property in question and its exact location when loss occurred.
  c. Time and manner of acquisition of claimant's ownership of the property or other interest therein.
  d. The action taken against the property which is considered as giving rise to a claim against a foreign government.
  e. Identification of persons, officials, agency, or forces taking such action and dates the action was taken.
  f. The nature and amount of damage resulting from action complained of.

Second: Statements of claimants in support of claims, even when under oath, must be corroborated by other evidence. Therefore, there should be attached to the sworn statement of claim, documentary evidence consisting of *original* documents or *certified copies* of originals, affidavits, etc., to support every essential allegation in the sworn statement. The documents filed as evidence should be numbered consecutively and cited by number immediately after the allegations in the sworn statement in support of which the documents are filed.

All evidence, as well as sworn statement, should be filed *in triplicate*.

Documents filed in other than the English language must be accompanied by authentic English translations.

If a claim involves losses in more than one country, a separate sworn statement of claim should be prepared with reference to damages sustained in *each* country.

Third: Nature of evidence required.
I. *Nationality.*
  A. *Of individuals.*
  1. If native-born:

Certified copy of birth certificate. If such certificate is unobtainable, and absence thereof is explained, claimant should furnish baptismal certificate or the affidavits of at least two persons (if affidavit of parent not obtainable) having personal knowledge of the facts, stating date and place of claimant's birth and basis of affiant's knowledge. Since citizenship of an American woman married prior to September 22, 1922 followed that of her husband, proof of the latter's citizenship must be furnished in such cases, together with a copy of the marriage certificate.

2. If naturalized:

Date and place of naturalization, designation of court and certificate number should be supplied.

Claimant should furnish same information to Immigration and Naturalization Service, Department of Justice, Washington, D.C., and request that Service to send to the Department of State evidence of such naturalization. Claimants having had communications from this Department with respect to their claims should also inform the Service of the Department's file number indicated on such correspondence, and request the Service to refer to such file number when furnishing this Department with information regarding the naturalization.

B. *Of American corporations, partnerships, or other forms of associations.*

1. Certified copy of charter or articles of incorporation, and of amendments thereto.

2. Certified copy of partnership agreement, and of amendments thereto.

3. Proof of citizenship of officers and directors of corporations or of partners should be supplied in manner indicated under I-A above.

4. Affidavit of officer of corporation as to citizenship of stockholders in so far as known should be furnished.

II. *Ownership of Property* (or other interest therein).

1. Certified copy of deeds, extracts from property registers, contract of purchase or other muniment of title should be submitted.

2. If obtained by inheritance, a certified copy of the decree of distribution and/or such other document or documents as may be necessary to establish succession should be furnished.

3. Any other evidence of a pertinent nature.

III. *Wrongful Acts Affecting the Property.*

1. Certified copy of any decree or order interfering with claimant's ownership of the property should be supplied.

2. Affidavits of persons having personal knowledge of wrongful action with respect to the property, setting out fully nature and date of such acts and by whom taken, should be supplied also.

2. Any other documentary evidence to establish action taken, such as requisition order, receipts for property taken, etc., should be included.

IV. *Proof of Damages Sustained.*

1. Contracts, deeds, vouchers, etc., showing original cost of property to claimant, constitute valuable evidence.

2. Same with respect to nature and cost of subsequent improvements.

3. Proof of nature and amount of income derived from the property for several years preceding the acts complained of.

4. Value of property at time of loss, including insured and tax valuations.

5. Extent to which depreciation has been taken into account in arriving at actual value.

6. Photographs, duly authenticated, where available, showing property and damage thereto.

7. Carefully itemized statement of losses sustained.

8. Affidavits of persons having personal knowledge of the property, the nature and amount of damages sustained and who are qualified to express reliable opinions as to the extent of damage.

9. Where a foreign currency enters into calculations mentioned above, the equivalent thereof in terms of U.S. currency should be stated, based upon the rate of exchange prevailing at the time in question. Final computation of loss should be made in U.S. currency at the rate of exchange in effect *at the time the loss occurred.*

10. Extent to which claimant has recovered through insurance or otherwise for property lost, destroyed, or damaged.

The foregoing should not be understood to comprehend all essential requirements in the preparation of a claim. The suggestions are offered simply as a guide for that purpose. Variation in the facts of particular cases may require special treatment and methods of proof. In general, all material allegations of a claimant must be supported by convincing evidence; otherwise, the claim may be disallowed for lack of proof.

A careful observance of these suggestions in preparing claims will facilitate, to a great extent, consideration of the claims by such agency as may be entrusted with that responsibility. It should be clearly understood that the responsibility for preparing their claims and obtaining appropriate evidence in support of allegations rests entirely with the claimants.

In cases in which claimants are represented by an attorney, the latter should file a power of attorney evidencing his authority to act in such capacity.

APPENDIX E

Memorandum in Relation to Evidence Necessary to
Establish American Nationality of Individuals

1. Proof of the American nationality of one requesting the assistance of the Department of State is essential.

2. If the American nationality is alleged by *virtue of birth in the United States*, it should be established by submitting an original or authenticated copy of an official birth certificate or a certified copy of the official records showing birth in the United States. In case neither of these is available, evidence to explain the reasons why they are not available should be submitted, accompanied by an authenticated copy of a baptismal registry, or by the affidavits of two or more persons having personal knowledge concerning *the time and place of birth*, which affidavits should *state specifically and clearly the facts which made it possible for the affiants to acquire such knowledge*. Birth or baptismal certificates to be acceptable must show that the birth or baptism was recorded shortly after birth. If nationality is alleged by *virtue of birth abroad to an American parent*, similar evidence relating to birth should be submitted, together with evidence establishing the American nationality of the parent.

3. If American nationality is alleged by *virtue of naturalization by a court*, a request in writing should be made to the Immigration and Naturalization Service, Department of Justice, Washington, D.C. to transmit evidence of the naturalization to the Office of the Legal Adviser, Department of State. In making such request, the name of the court granting citizenship and the date of the court's action should be given.

4. If American nationality is alleged through the naturalization of a parent, application should be made to the Immigration and Naturalization Service, Department of Justice, Washington, D.C., for a certificate of derivative citizenship. When the certificate is obtained the Service should be requested to transmit evidence of the derivative naturalization to the Office of the Legal Adviser, Department of State.

5. If American Nationality, on behalf of a married woman, is al-

leged by *virtue of marriage to an American citizen prior to September 22, 1922,* evidence with respect to the husband's nationality should be submitted in accordance with paragraphs 2 or 3 above, together with a certified copy of the marriage certificate and an affidavit setting forth what changes, if any, have occurred in the marital status since marriage. In case the marriage occurred after September 22, 1922, a complete statement of the facts should be submitted to the Department, which will then give advice as to the evidence required.

6. If American nationality is claimed through any other process than above stated, the Department should be furnished with a full statement of the facts.

Memorandum in Relation to Evidence Necessary to Establish the American Nationality of Corporations, Joint Stock Companies and Partnerships

In submitting evidence of the nationality of American concerns, the following material should be furnished:

A. *Corporations and Joint Stock Companies*

1. Certified copies of the articles of incorporation and all amendments thereto, clearly establishing the status of the corporation. (In cases of joint stock companies there should be submitted certified copies of the articles of organization or articles of agreement, and amendments.) Copies of articles of incorporation, etc., should be authenticated by the appropriate state official, usually the Secretary of State of the state of incorporation.

2. An affidavit by the proper officer of the concern giving the names and nationality of the officers and directors and, to the extent such information is available, the nationality of the principal shareholders, and the number of shares owned by each.

B. *Partnerships*

1. Certified copies of the partnership agreement and all amendments thereto, clearly establishing the status of the partnership at the time the claim arose and from that time, continuously, until the submission of the claim.

2. An affidavit by the proper officer of the partnership, giving the names and nationality of the officers and partners, and their respective interests in the partnership.

3. Evidence of the American nationality of all American citizens who are members of the partnership. (See the . . . [prior memorandum] in relation to evidence necessary to establish American nationality of individuals.)

APPENDIX F

ARTICLE 1

Seat of the Commission

The United States–Japanese Property Commission constituted between the United States of America and Japan (hereinafter called the Commission) under "The Agreement for the Settlement of Disputes Arising under Article 15(a) of the Treaty of Peace with Japan" shall have its seat at Tokyo.

ARTICLE 2

Jurisdiction

A. The Commission shall have jurisdiction over all disputes between the United States of America and Japan which may have arisen in the interpretation and execution of Article 15(a) of the Treaty of Peace with Japan, and have been referred to the Commission pursuant to Article 1 of "The Agreement for the Settlement of Disputes arising under Article 15(a) of the Treaty of Peace with Japan," it being understood that the draft Allied Powers Property Compensation Law approved by the Japanese Cabinet on July 13, 1951 and subsequently enacted as the Allied Powers Property Compensation Law (Law 264 of 1951) is part of the contents of Article 15(a).

B. The Commission shall decide whether it has jurisdiction over a dispute which has been referred to it for determination.

ARTICLE 3

Sittings

A. No sitting of the Commission shall be held unless all the members are present, except as provided in paragraph B. The rulings and decisions of the Commission shall be rendered upon the concurrence of a majority of the members.

B. The members appointed by the Government of the United States of American and the Government of Japan may, in the absence from Japan of the third member, and if they are in agreement, make a ruling on behalf of the Commission on any question of a procedural nature.

C. The sittings of the Commission will be held at such places in Japan and at such times as the members may from time to time agree upon.

ARTICLE 4

Definitions

The word "Ruling" as used in the present Rules of Procedure shall refer to any ruling, order or other measure taken by the Commission of an interim character which does not relate to the merits of the dispute. The word "Decision" shall refer to the written record of any determination of the Commission affecting the merits of the dispute. The word "Pleading" shall be deemed to include a Petition, an Answer, a Reply and a Counter-Reply.

ARTICLE 5

Languages

A. The official languages of the Commission shall be English and Japanese.

B. Request for Rulings, Pleadings, and other similar documents, may be submitted in either English or Japanese. Supporting statements, affidavits, and other documentary evidence may be submitted in any language. If, however, such evidence is in a language other than the language of the Party presenting the evidence, a translation shall be attached.

C. Oral proceedings before the Commission may be held in either English or Japanese.

D. The Rulings and Decisions of the Commission and its Register and Minutes shall be in English and Japanese.

ARTICLE 6

Parties and Agents

A. The Parties before the Commission shall be the Government of the United States of America and the Government of Japan.

B. Each Party shall be represented before the Commission by an Agent. The Agent may be assisted by one or more Deputy Agents. The Party concerned shall notify to the Commission and to the other Party the names of such Agents and Deputy Agents. The term "Agent" as used in the present Rules of Procedure shall be deemed to include a duly appointed Deputy Agent.

C. Persons on whose behalf the proceedings are initiated or persons interested in a dispute, shall not be appointed Agents. Such restriction shall not, however, apply to attorneys who have not acted in a case before its reference to the Commission as a dispute between the Parties.

ARTICLE 7

Secretariat

A. The Commission shall establish a Secretariat which shall be under the direction of a Secretary General to be selected by the Commission. The Secretary General may, with the approval of the Commission, and within the limits of available funds, appoint such assistants and clerks as may be required by him.

B. The Secretariat shall:

1. Keep a Register in which shall be entered the information enumerated below:
    a) The name of the case before the Commission;
    b) The name and address of the person, whether physical or juridical, on whose behalf the proceedings are initiated;
    c) The date of the presentation of each Request for a Ruling, Pleading, and other similar document;
    d) The substance of the Rulings and Decisions made by the Commission;
    e) Such other matters as the Commission may prescribe;
2. Receive at the Secretariat Requests for Rulings, Pleadings and the written evidence pertaining to a dispute, as well as all other documents relating thereto;
3. Stamp every copy with the date of its receipt;
4. File the original in the archives of the Secretariat;
5. Translate the material received into the language of the opposite Party;
6. Transmit a copy and translation to each member of the Commission except as may be otherwise arranged;
7. Transmit a copy and translation to the Agent of each Party;
8. Take minutes of the progress and results of the proceedings of the Commission;
9. Provide such other interpreting and translating services as may be required by the Commission;
10. Attend to such other matters as may be prescribed by the Commission.

Article 8

Seal of the Commission

The Commission shall have its seal which shall be in the custody of the Secretary General. All notices, orders and other documents sealed with the Seal of the Commission shall be presumed to be official.

Article 9

Inspection and Copying of Documents

The Agent of either Party may inspect and copy at the Secretariat the original of a Request for a Ruling, Pleading, and other similar document, and of the evidence relating to a dispute submitted to the Commission.

Article 10

Petition

A. The proceedings before the Commission shall be initiated by the filing of a Petition by the Agent of the Government of the United States of America.

B. The Petition shall contain in separate paragraphs:

1. The name, address and nationality of the physical or juridical person on whose behalf the proceedings are initiated, and in the case of a juridical person, the qualification of such a person to receive the relief requested from the Commission:

2. The name, address and nationality of the legal representative, if any, of the person on whose behalf the proceedings are initiated, together with documentary evidence of the authority of such legal representative to act on behalf of his principal:

3. A clear and concise statement of the facts in the dispute with each material allegation set forth insofar as possible in a separate paragraph:

4. A clear and concise statement of the legal grounds upon which the responsibility of the Government of Japan is alleged:

5. A complete statement setting forth the reason why the Government of the United States of America has not been satisfied with the action taken by the Government of Japan under Article 15(a) of the Treaty of Peace with Japan with respect to the dispute referred to the Commission and the relief required, including, if any, the amount of compensation claimed.

Article 11

Answer

A. Within three months after the date of the filing of the Petition, the Answer to the petition shall be filed by the Agent of the Government of Japan which Answer shall contain:

1. A clear and concise statement of the facts presented in the Petition of the Government of the United States of America which are admitted as true by the Government of Japan;
2. A clear and concise statement of any other element of fact upon which the Government of Japan is relying for its defense of the case;
3. A clear and concise statement of the legal grounds upon which the responsibility of the Government of Japan is denied.

B. The Agent of the Government of Japan may, at his option, refrain from setting forth the amount of damage the Government of Japan considers would be payable in the event its responsibility were established, and may confine himself to a general statement questioning the appropriateness of the amount claimed.

Article 12

Reply and Counter-Reply

A. The Agent of the Government of the United States of America may file a Reply with the Secretariat within three months after the date of the filing of the Answer.

B. The Agent of the Government of Japan may file a Counter-Reply with the Secretariat within three months after the date of the filing of the Reply.

Article 13

Evidence

A. Evidence shall be submitted simultaneously with the filing of the pleadings. The Commission may nevertheless, upon good cause shown, authorize the submission of additional evidence at any time before the proceedings are concluded. Such additional evidence may be either written or oral. Oral evidence shall, however, be submitted only in those instances where the presentation of oral testimony would be advantageous to the consideration of the dispute by the Commission. If the Commission authorizes the submission of evidence by one Party additional to that submitted with the Pleadings, it shall make adequate provision to permit the submission of rebuttal evidence by the other Party.

B. The Commission shall be free to determine the probative value of the evidence submitted.

C. Except as otherwise specifically provided or authorized by the Commission all written evidence shall be presented in original and five copies.

D. The Commission may, on its own initiative, or at the request of the Agent of either Party and for good cause shown, examine a witness present in Japan. The witness shall, before testifying, take an oath in accordance with the practice of his country. The witness may be cross-examined by the Agent of the Party against which the witness renders testimony.

E. The Commission may appoint an expert and request him to submit an opinion in writing on any factual matter pertinent to the dispute. The Commission may, on its own initiative, and shall, at the request of the Agent of either Party, summon the expert to appear before the Commission. The expert may be challenged or cross-examined by the Agent of the Party against which the expert renders testimony.

ARTICLE 14

Argument and Explanation

The Commission may, on its own initiative or at the request of either Agent, call on either or both Agents for an oral or written argument, or an oral or written explanation on particular factual or legal matters pertinent to the dispute.

ARTICLE 15

Time Periods

A. The Commission may, at the request of the interested Agent, extend in its discretion the period for the filing of any Pleading or other similar document when it is established to its satisfaction that the time provided by the present Rules of Procedure, or by a Ruling of the Commission, is insufficient.

B. Whenever, under the present Rules of Procedure, or by a Ruling of the Commission, a certain period is fixed for the accomplishment of a procedural act, the date from which the period begins to run shall not be counted, but the last day of the period shall be counted. If the last day falls on a Sunday, or on a legal holiday of either Party, the following day shall be the last day.

ARTICLE 16

Submission and Signing of Pleadings and Other Documents

All Requests for Rulings, Pleadings, and other similar documents, shall be submitted in original and five copies, each of which shall be signed by the Agent on behalf of this [sic] Government.

ARTICLE 17

Assistance to the Commission

Each Government shall afford all possible assistance to the Commission at its request, and shall, in particular take all possible measures to provide for the attendance of witnesses present in Japan and for the production of documents.

ARTICLE 18

Withdrawal of Pleading

At any stage of the proceedings, the Government of the United States of America may withdraw the Petition, or the Government of Japan may withdraw the Answer. In such event the Commission shall make a determination in favor of the opposite Party.

ARTICLE 19

Compromise

A. The Commission may try to effect a compromise at any stage of the proceedings.

B. When a compromise is reached, the Commission shall render a Decision setting forth the terms of the compromise and declaring the dispute settled.

ARTICLE 20

Decision

A. The Decision shall contain:
1. A declaration of the Commission's jurisdiction;
2. The name of the person on whose behalf the proceedings have been initiated;
3. The object of the dispute;

4. A statement of the material facts and legal arguments;

5. The determination and the grounds therefor, affirming or denying, in whole, or in part, the relief requested;

6. The signatures of the members of the Commission concurring in the Decision and the date such Decision is adopted.

B. The Decision shall be deposited with the Secretariat, which shall furnish certified true copies thereof immediately to the Agent of each Party.

C. The Decision shall be definitive and binding on the two Parties.

D. Where the determination relates solely to one or more points of law or fact and is not finally determinative of the dispute, the Decision shall contain only as many of the points listed under paragraph "A" as are relevant to the Decision.

E. Where a determination is made of all issues of law of fact other than those relating to the amount of compensation, and the responsibility of the Government of Japan has been established, the Parties shall have one month from the date of such determination to reach agreement as to a mutually agreeable sum. In the event the Parties are unable to agree upon such a sum, the Agent of the Government of Japan shall, within an additional period of two months, submit to the Commission a Statement setting forth the amount of compensation the Government of Japan considers to be due in payment of the claim. Such Statement shall be supported by appropriate written evidence.

F. The Commission shall render a determination with respect to the amount of compensation as soon as possible following the filing of such a Statement. If not satisfied with the evidence submitted with the Petition or the Statement, the Commission may call for additional evidence, oral or written, in accordance with the present Rules of Procedure.

ARTICLE 21

Minority Opinion

If a determination is not reached with unanimity, the member in the minority may state his views in a Minority Opinion.

ARTICLE 22

Costs

Each Party shall bear its own costs of the proceedings.

ARTICLE 23

Amendments and Derogations

A. The Commission shall have the right at any time to amend or complete the present Rules of Procedure either by a unanimous or by a majority decision.

B. The Commission may, in a specific case where both Parties agree, depart from the present Rules of Procedure.

Done in the English and Japanese languages, both equally authentic, and adopted on the 31st day of March 1959.

Third Member

United States Member   Japanese Member

Bibliography

Bibliographical Note: This working bibliography was selected with the private and governmental lawyer in mind. It contains those entries most helpful to persons who must prepare and present international claims. Older and less useful entries have been omitted, but it is believed that the bibliography is sufficiently comprehensive to be of substantial value to all students of international law.

The bibliography, with the exception of several English entries, is limited in scope to American materials. It is divided into three headings: source materials (consisting of opinions and reports of various claims commissions), books, and articles appearing in legal periodicals. Further references, not included in the bibliography, may be found in the footnotes throughout the book.

SOURCE MATERIALS

AMERICAN-MEXICAN CLAIMS COMMISSION. REPORT TO THE SECRETARY OF STATE. Washington, D.C.: United States Government Printing Office, 1948.

BONYNGE, ROBERT W. REPORT OF AGENT BEFORE THE MIXED CLAIMS COMMISSION, UNITED STATES AND GERMANY. Washington, D.C.: United States Government Printing Office, 1935.

———. REPORT OF AGENT BEFORE THE TRIPARTITE CLAIM COMMISSION (UNITED STATES, AUSTRIA, AND HUNGARY). Washington, D.C.: United States Government Printing Office, 1930.

FINAL REPORT OF THE COMMISSIONER AND DECISIONS AND OPINIONS, TRIPARTITE CLAIMS COMMISSION (UNITED STATES, AUSTRIA, AND HUNGARY). Washington, D.C.: United States Government Printing Office, 1933.

FINAL REPORT OF THE SPANISH TREATY CLAIMS COMMISSION. Washington, D.C.: United States Government Printing Office, 1910.

FOREIGN CLAIMS SETTLEMENT COMMISSION. FIRST THROUGH FOURTEENTH SEMIANNUAL REPORTS (1954–1961).

HUNT, BERT L. REPORT OF THE AMERICAN AND PANAMANIAN GENERAL CLAIMS ARBITRATION. Washington, D.C.: United States Government Printing Office, 1934.

INTERNATIONAL CLAIMS COMMISSION. FIRST THROUGH EIGHTH SEMIANNUAL REPORTS (1950–1954).

MARTIN, H. H. FINAL REPORT OF AGENT BEFORE THE MIXED CLAIMS COMMISSION, UNITED STATES AND GERMANY. Washington, D.C.: United States Government Printing Office, 1941.

MIXED CLAIMS COMMISSION, UNITED STATES AND GERMANY, ADMINISTRATIVE DECISIONS AND OPINIONS OF A GENERAL NATURE AND OPINIONS IN INDIVIDUAL LUSITANIA CLAIMS AND OTHER CASES TO OCTOBER 1, 1926. Washington, D.C.: United States Government Printing Office, 1928.

MIXED CLAIMS COMMISSION, UNITED STATES AND GERMANY, ADMINISTRATIVE DECISIONS AND OPINIONS OF A GENERAL NATURE AND OPINIONS AND DECISIONS IN CERTAIN INDIVIDUAL CLAIMS FROM OCTOBER 1, 1926 TO DECEMBER 31, 1932. Washington, D.C.: United States Government Printing Office, 1933.

MIXED CLAIMS COMMISSION, UNITED STATES AND GERMANY, OPINIONS AND DECISIONS FROM JANUARY 1, 1933 TO OCTOBER 31, 1939 (EXCEPTING DECISIONS IN THE SABOTAGE CLAIMS OF JUNE 15 AND

October 30, 1939). Washington, D.C.: United States Government Printing Office, 1939.

Moore, John Bassett. History and Digest of the International Arbitrations to which the United States has been a party. 6 vols. Washington, D.C.: United States Government Printing Office, 1898.

———. International Adjudications, Modern Series. 6 vols. New York: Oxford University Press, 1929–1933.

Nielsen, Frederick Kenelm. American and British Claims Arbitration. Washington, D.C.: United States Government Printing Office, 1926.

———. American-Turkish Claims Settlement, Opinions and Report. Washington, D.C.: United States Government Printing Office, 1937.

Opinions of Commissioners under the Convention Concluded September 8, 1923, between the United States and Mexico. Washington, D.C.: United States Government Printing Office, 1927.

Opinions of Commissioners under the Convention Concluded September 8, 1923, as Extended by the Convention Signed August 16, 1927 between the United States and Mexico. Washington, D.C.: United States Government Printing Office, 1929.

Opinions of Commissioners under the Convention Concluded September 8, 1923, as Extended by Subsequent Conventions between the United States and Mexico. Washington, D.C.: United States Government Printing Office, 1931.

Opinions of Commissioners under the Convention Concluded September 10, 1923 between the United States and Mexico, as Extended by the Convention concluded August 17, 1929. Washington, D.C.: United States Government Printing Office, 1931.

Ralston, Jackson H. French-Venezuelan Mixed Claims Commission of 1902. Washington, D.C.: United States Government Printing Office, 1906.

———. Venezuelan Arbitrations of 1903. Washington, D.C.: United States Government Printing Office, 1904.

REPORTS OF INTERNATIONAL ARBITRAL AWARDS. United Nations. 10 vols.

SALEM CLAIM (CLAIM OF THE UNITED STATES OF AMERICA ON BEHALF OF GEORGE J. SALEM V. THE ROYAL GOVERNMENT OF EGYPT). Washington, D.C.: United States Government Printing Office, 1933.

SETTLEMENT OF CLAIMS BY THE FOREIGN CLAIMS SETTLEMENT COMMISSION OF THE UNITED STATES AND ITS PREDECESSORS, 1949–1955. Washington, D.C.: United States Government Printing Office, 1955.

SHUFELDT CLAIM (CLAIM OF THE UNITED STATES OF AMERICA ON BEHALF OF P. W. SHUFELDT V. THE REPUBLIC OF GUATEMALA). Washington, D.C.: United States Government Printing Office, 1932.

SPECIAL MEXICAN CLAIMS COMMISSION. REPORT TO THE SECRETARY OF STATE. Washington, D.C.: United States Government Printing Office, 1940.

SPECIAL REPORT OF WILLIAM E. FULLER. Washington, D.C.: United States Government Printing Office, 1907.

WAR CLAIMS COMMISSION. FIRST THROUGH TENTH SEMIANNUAL REPORTS (1950–1954).

BOOKS

AMERICAN LAW INSTITUTE. RESTATEMENT OF THE LAW: THE FOREIGN RELATIONS LAW OF THE UNITED STATES: PROPOSED OFFICIAL DRAFT. Philadelphia, Pa.: American Law Institute, 1962.

BAR-YAACOV, NISSIM. DUAL NATIONALITY. New York: Frederick A. Praeger, 1961.

BISHOP, JR., WILLIAM W. INTERNATIONAL LAW CASES AND MATERIALS. Second Edition. Boston, Mass.: Little, Brown & Co., 1962.

BORCHARD, EDWIN M. THE DIPLOMATIC PROTECTION OF CITIZENS ABROAD. New York: The Banks Law Publishing Co., 1916.

BRIERLY, J. L. THE LAW OF NATIONS. Fifth Edition. London: Oxford University Press, 1955.

BRIGGS, HERBERT WITTAKER. THE LAW OF NATIONS: CASES, DOCUMENTS AND NOTES. Second Edition. New York: Appleton-Century-Crofts, Inc., 1952.

———. THE PUNITIVE NATURE OF DAMAGES IN INTERNATIONAL LAW AND STATE RESPONSIBILITY FOR FAILURE TO APPREHEND, PROSECUTE, OR PUNISH. Baltimore, Md.: Johns Hopkins Press, 1937.

CARLSTON, KENNETH SMITH. THE PROCESS OF INTERNATIONAL ARBITRATION. New York: Columbia University Press, 1946.

CHENG, BIN. GENERAL PRINCIPLES OF LAW AS APPLIED BY INTERNATIONAL COURTS AND TRIBUNALS. London: Stevens & Sons, Ltd., 1953.

DE BEUS, J. G. THE JURISPRUDENCE OF THE GENERAL CLAIMS COMMISSION, UNITED STATES AND MEXICO UNDER THE CONVENTION OF SEPTEMBER 8, 1923. The Hague: Martinus Nijhoff, 1938.

DOMKE, MARTIN (Editor). INTERNATIONAL TRADE ARBITRATION. New York: American Arbitration Association, 1958.

DUNN, FREDERICK SHERWOOD. THE DIPLOMATIC PROTECTION OF AMERICANS IN MEXICO. New York: Columbia University Press, 1933.

———. THE PROTECTION OF NATIONALS: A STUDY IN THE APPLICATION OF INTERNATIONAL LAW. Baltimore, Md.: Johns Hopkins Press, 1932.

EAGLETON, CLYDE. THE RESPONSIBILITY OF STATES IN INTERNATIONAL LAW. New York: New York University Press, 1928.

FELLER, ABRAHAM HOWARD. THE MEXICAN CLAIMS COMMISSIONS. New York: The Macmillan Co., 1935.

FENWICK, CHARLES G. INTERNATIONAL LAW. Third Edition. New York: Appleton-Century-Crofts, Inc., 1948.

FOIGHEL, ISI. NATIONALIZATION. London: Stevens & Sons, Ltd., 1957.

FREEMAN, ALWYN VERNON. THE INTERNATIONAL RESPONSIBILITY OF STATES FOR DENIAL OF JUSTICE. New York: Longmans, Green & Co., 1938.

FRIEDMAN, SAMY. EXPROPRIATION IN INTERNATIONAL LAW. London: Stevens & Sons, Ltd., 1953.

GOLDSCHMIDT, S. LEGAL CLAIMS AGAINST GERMANY. New York: The Dryden Press, 1945.

153

HACKWORTH, GREEN HAYWOOD. A DIGEST OF INTERNATIONAL LAW. Vol. 5. Washington, D.C.: United States Government Printing Office, 1943.

HUDSON, MANLEY O. INTERNATIONAL TRIBUNALS. Washington, D.C.: Carnegie Endowment for International Peace and Brookings Institution, 1944.

HYDE, CHARLES CHENEY. INTERNATIONAL LAW CHIEFLY AS INTERPRETED AND APPLIED BY THE UNITED STATES. Second Edition of Vol. 1. Boston, Mass.: Little, Brown & Co., 1945.

JESSUP, PHILIP C. A MODERN LAW OF NATIONS. New York: The Macmillan Co., 1948.

———. THE USE OF INTERNATIONAL LAW. Ann Arbor, Mich.: The University of Michigan Law School, 1959.

KIESSELBACH, WILHELM J. PROBLEMS OF THE GERMAN-AMERICAN CLAIMS COMMISSION. Washington, D.C.: Carnegie Endowment for International Peace, 1930.

LILLICH, RICHARD B. INTERNATIONAL CLAIMS: THEIR ADJUDICATION BY NATIONAL COMMISSIONS. Syracuse, N.Y.: Syracuse University Press, 1962.

MOORE, JOHN BASSETT. A DIGEST OF INTERNATIONAL LAW. Vol. 6. Washington, D.C.: United States Government Printing Office, 1906.

NIELSEN, FREDERICK KENELM. INTERNATIONAL LAW APPLIED TO RECLAMATIONS. Washington, D.C.: John Byrne & Co., 1933.

OPPENHEIM, LASSA F. L. INTERNATIONAL LAW, A TREATISE. Seventh Edition of Vol. 2, Lauterpacht. London, New York, Toronto: Longmans, Green & Co., 1952.

RALSTON, JACKSON HARVEY. INTERNATIONAL ARBITRATION FROM ATHENS TO LOCARNO. Stanford, Calif.: Stanford University Press, 1929.

———. THE LAW AND PROCEDURE OF INTERNATIONAL TRIBUNALS. Stanford, Calif.: Stanford University Press, 1926.

———. SUPPLEMENT TO THE LAW AND PROCEDURE OF INTERNATIONAL TRIBUNALS. Stanford, Calif.: Stanford University Press, 1936.

RE, EDWARD DOMENIC. FOREIGN CONFISCATIONS IN ANGLO-AMERICAN LAW. New York: Oceana Publications, 1951.

ROTH, A. H. THE MINIMUM STANDARD OF INTERNATIONAL LAW APPLIED TO ALIENS. Leiden: 1950.

RUBIN, SEYMOUR. PRIVATE FOREIGN INVESTMENT. Baltimore, Md.: The Johns Hopkins Press, 1956.

SANDIFER, DURWARD V. EVIDENCE BEFORE INTERNATIONAL TRIBUNALS. Chicago, Ill.: The Foundation Press, Inc., 1939.

SCHWARZENBERGER, GEORG. A MANUAL OF INTERNATIONAL LAW. Fourth Edition of Vol. 1. New York: Frederick A. Praeger, 1960.

———. INTERNATIONAL LAW AS APPLIED BY INTERNATIONAL COURTS AND TRIBUNALS. Third Edition of Vol. 1. London: Stevens & Sons, Ltd., 1957.

SHEA, DONALD R. THE CALVO CLAUSE. Minneapolis, Minn.: University of Minnesota Press, 1955.

SILVANIE, HAIG. RESPONSIBILITY OF STATES FOR ACTS OF UNSUCCESSFUL INSURGENT GOVERNMENTS. New York: Columbia University Press, 1939.

SIMPSON, J. L., and FOX, HAZEL. INTERNATIONAL ARBITRATION. New York: Frederick A. Praeger, 1959.

STUYT, A. M. SURVEY OF INTERNATIONAL ARBITRATIONS 1794–1938. The Hague: Martinus Nijhoff, 1939.

THORPE, GORDON CYRUS. PREPARATION OF INTERNATIONAL CLAIMS. St. Paul, Minn.: West Publishing Co., 1924.

WHITE, GILLIAN. NATIONALISATION OF FOREIGN PROPERTY. London: Stevens & Sons, Ltd., 1961.

WHITEMAN, MARJORIE MILLACE. DAMAGES IN INTERNATIONAL LAW. 3 vols. Washington, D.C.: United States Government Printing Office, 1937–1943.

WILSON, GEORGE GRAFTON. HANDBOOK OF INTERNATIONAL LAW. Third Edition. St. Paul, Minn.: West Publishing Co., 1939.

WORMSER, RENÉ ALBERT. COLLECTION OF INTERNATIONAL WAR DAMAGE CLAIMS. New York: The Alexander Publishing Co., Inc., 1944.

WORTLEY, B. A. EXPROPRIATION IN PUBLIC INTERNATIONAL LAW. Cambridge, England: The University Press, 1959.

ARTICLES

ABDEL-WAHAB, SALAH-ELDIN. *Economic Development Agreements and Nationalization.* 30 UNIVERSITY OF CINCINNATI LAW REVIEW 418 (1961).

ANDERSON, CHANDLER P. *Basis of the Law Against Confiscating Foreign-Owned Property.* 21 AMERICAN JOURNAL OF INTERNATIONAL LAW 525 (1927).

ANDERSON, J. N. D. *The Moslem Ruler and Contractual Obligations.* 33 NEW YORK UNIVERSITY LAW REVIEW 917 (1958).

ARIAS, HARMODIO. *The Non-Liability of States for Damage Suffered by Foreigners in the Course of a Riot, an Insurrection, or a Civil War.* 7 AMERICAN JOURNAL OF INTERNATIONAL LAW 724 (1913).

BAADE, HANS W. *Indonesian Nationalization Measures Before Foreign Courts—A Reply.* 54 AMERICAN JOURNAL OF INTERNATIONAL LAW 801 (1960).

BAGGE, ALGOT. *Intervention on the Ground of Damage Caused to Nationals, with Particular Reference to Exhaustion of Local Remedies and the Rights of Shareholders.* 34 BRITISH YEARBOOK OF INTERNATIONAL LAW 162 (1958).

BECKER, LOFTUS E. *Just Compensation in Expropriation Cases: Decline and Partial Recovery.* 53 AMERICAN SOCIETY OF INTERNATIONAL LAW PROCEEDINGS 336 (1959).

BECKETT, W. E. *Diplomatic Claims in Respect to Injuries to Companies,* IN 17 TRANSACTIONS OF THE GROTIUS SOCIETY 175 (1931).

BERMAN, NANETTE D. *Property Claims Arising from Germany's Wartime Occupations: Shall They be Decided in Accordance with International Law?* 8 FEDERAL BAR JOURNAL 277, 357 (1947), 9 FEDERAL BAR JOURNAL 169 (1948).

BONSAL, DUDLEY B. *International Claims: A Lawyer's View on a Diplomat's Nightmare.* 49 AMERICAN SOCIETY OF INTERNATIONAL LAW PROCEEDINGS 63 (1955).

BORCHARD, EDWIN M. *Basic Elements of Diplomatic Protection of*

Citizens Abroad. 7 AMERICAN JOURNAL OF INTERNATIONAL LAW 497 (1913).

———. *Confiscations: Extraterritorial and Domestic.* 31 AMERICAN JOURNAL OF INTERNATIONAL LAW 675 (1937).

———. *Contractual Claims in International Law.* 13 COLUMBIA LAW REVIEW 457 (1913).

———. *Extraterritorial Confiscations.* 36 AMERICAN JOURNAL OF INTERNATIONAL LAW 275 (1942).

———. *Nationalization of Enemy Patents.* 37 AMERICAN JOURNAL OF INTERNATIONAL LAW 92 (1943).

———. *"Responsibility of States," at the Hague Codification Conference.* 24 AMERICAN JOURNAL OF INTERNATIONAL LAW 517 (1930).

———. *Responsibility of States for Damage Done in Their Territories to the Person or Property of Foreigners.* 20 AMERICAN JOURNAL OF INTERNATIONAL LAW 738 (1926).

———. *The Local Remedy Rule.* 28 AMERICAN JOURNAL OF INTERNATIONAL LAW 729 (1934).

———. *The "Minimum Standard" of the Treatment of Aliens.* 38 MICHIGAN LAW REVIEW 445 (1940).

———. *The Protection of Citizens Abroad and Change of Original Nationality.* 43 YALE LAW JOURNAL 359 (1934).

BRANDON, MICHAEL. *Recent Measures to Improve the International Investment Climate.* 9 JOURNAL OF PUBLIC LAW 125 (1960).

BRIERLY, J. L. *The Theory of Implied State Complicity in International Claims.* 1928 BRITISH YEARBOOK OF INTERNATIONAL LAW 42.

BRIGGS, HERBERT WITTAKER. *The Local Remedies Rule: A Drafting Suggestion.* 50 AMERICAN JOURNAL OF INTERNATIONAL LAW 921 (1956).

———. *The Settlement of Mexican Claims Act of 1942.* 37 AMERICAN JOURNAL OF INTERNATIONAL LAW 222 (1943).

CARDOZO, MICHAEL H. *Attempts to Transmute Indemnity into Discharge of Claims in Executive Agreements.* 49 AMERICAN JOURNAL OF INTERNATIONAL LAW 560 (1955).

CARLSTON, KENNETH S. *Codification of International Arbitral Proce-*

dures. 47 AMERICAN JOURNAL OF INTERNATIONAL LAW 203 (1953).

———. *Concession Agreements and Nationalization.* 52 AMERICAN JOURNAL OF INTERNATIONAL LAW 260 (1958).

———. *International Role of Concession Agreements.* 52 NORTH-WESTERN UNIVERSITY LAW REVIEW 618 (1958).

———. *Nationalization: An Analytical Approach.* 54 NORTHWESTERN UNIVERSITY LAW REVIEW 405 (1959).

CHRISTENSON, GORDON A. *The United States–Rumanian Claims Settlement Agreement of March 30, 1960.* 55 AMERICAN JOURNAL OF INTERNATIONAL LAW 617 (1961).

———. *International Claims Procedure Before the Department of State.* 13 SYRACUSE LAW REVIEW 527 (1962).

CLARK, JR., JOSHUA REUBEN. *Legal Aspects Regarding the Owner-ship and Distribution of Awards.* 7 AMERICAN JOURNAL OF INTER-NATIONAL LAW 382 (1913).

CLAY, HENRY J. *Aspects of Settling Claims under the Yugoslav Claims Agreement of 1948.* 43 GEORGETOWN LAW JOURNAL 582 (1955).

———. *Recent Developments in the Protection of American Share-holders' Interests in Foreign Corporations.* 45 GEORGETOWN LAW JOURNAL 1 (1956).

———. *Relief for War Victims: Recent Foreign Claims Legislation.* 42 AMERICAN BAR ASSOCIATION JOURNAL 337 (1956).

COERPER, MILO G. *The Foreign Claims Settlement Commission and Judicial Review.* 50 AMERICAN JOURNAL OF INTERNATIONAL LAW 868 (1956).

COUDERT, FREDERIC R. *The Mexican Situation and Protection of American Property Abroad.* 24 AMERICAN BAR ASSOCIATION JOUR-NAL 813 (1938).

COULSON, N. J. *The Moslem Ruler and Contractual Obligations.* 33 NEW YORK UNIVERSITY LAW REVIEW 917 (1958).

COWLES, WILLARD B. *Review of the United Nations Charter and the Adjudication of International Claims.* 48 AMERICAN JOURNAL OF INTERNATIONAL LAW 460 (1954).

——. *To What Extent Will American Lawyers Need an Understanding of International Law To Serve Clients Adequately During the Last Half of the Twentieth Century?* 7 JOURNAL OF LEGAL EDUCATION 179 (1954).

CRANDALL, SAMUEL B. *Principles of International Law Applied by the Spanish Treaty Claims Commission.* 4 AMERICAN JOURNAL OF INTERNATIONAL LAW 806 (1910).

DAYTON, DOUGLAS E. *Comment.* 49 AMERICAN SOCIETY OF INTERNATIONAL LAW PROCEEDINGS 80 (1955).

DELSON, ROBERT. *Nationalization of the Suez Canal Company: Issues of Public and Private International Law.* 57 COLUMBIA LAW REVIEW 755 (1957).

DOMAN, NICHOLAS R. *Postwar Nationalization of Foreign Property in Europe.* 48 COLUMBIA LAW REVIEW 1125 (1948).

DOMKE, MARTIN. *American Protection Against Foreign Expropriation in the Light of the Suez Canal Crisis.* 105 UNIVERSITY OF PENNSYLVANIA LAW REVIEW 1033 (1957).

——. *Foreign Nationalizations.* 55 AMERICAN JOURNAL OF INTERNATIONAL LAW 585 (1961).

——. *Indonesian Nationalization Measures Before Foreign Courts.* 54 AMERICAN JOURNAL OF INTERNATIONAL LAW 305 (1960).

——. *International Arbitration of Commercial Disputes,* IN 2 INSTITUTE ON PRIVATE INVESTMENT ABROAD 131 (1960).

——. *On the Nationalization of Foreign Shareholders' Interests.* 4 NEW YORK LAW FORUM 46 (1958).

——. *"Piercing the Corporate Veil" in the Law of Economic Warfare.* 1955 WISCONSIN LAW REVIEW 77.

——. *The Settlement of International Investment Disputes.* 12 BUSINESS LAWYER 264 (1957).

DOWNEY, JR., WILLIAM GERALD. *Claims for Reparations and Damages Resulting from Violation of Neutral Rights.* 16 LAW AND CONTEMPORARY PROBLEMS 487 (1951).

DRAGO, LUIS M. *State Loans in Their Relation to International Policy.* 1 AMERICAN JOURNAL OF INTERNATIONAL LAW 692 (1907).

DRUCKER, ALFRED. *Compensation for Nationalized Property: The*

British Practice. 49 AMERICAN JOURNAL OF INTERNATIONAL LAW 477 (1955).

———. *Compensation Treaties Between Communist States.* 10 INTERNATIONAL AND COMPARATIVE LAW QUARTERLY 238 (1961).

———. *The Nationalisation of United Nations Property in Europe,* IN 36 TRANSACTIONS OF THE GROTIUS SOCIETY 75 (1951).

DUNN, FREDERICK SHERWOOD. *International Law and Private Property Rights.* 28 COLUMBIA LAW REVIEW 166 (1928).

EAGLETON, CLYDE. *Measure of Damages in International Law.* 39 YALE LAW JOURNAL 52 (1929).

FACHIRI, ALEXANDER P. *Expropriation and International Law.* 1925 BRITISH YEARBOOK OF INTERNATIONAL LAW 159.

———. *International Law and the Property of Aliens.* 1929 BRITISH YEARBOOK OF INTERNATIONAL LAW 32.

———. *The Local Remedies Rule in the Light of the Finnish Ships Arbitration.* 17 BRITISH YEARBOOK OF INTERNATIONAL LAW 19 (1936).

FAWCETT, J. E. S. *Some Foreign Effects of Nationalization of Property.* 27 BRITISH YEARBOOK OF INTERNATIONAL LAW 355 (1950).

———. *The Exhaustion of Local Remedies: Substance or Procedure?* 31 BRITISH YEARBOOK OF INTERNATIONAL LAW 452 (1954).

FEHR, JOSEPH CONRAD. *International Law As Applied by U.S.–Mexico Claims Commission.* 14 AMERICAN BAR ASSOCIATION JOURNAL 312 (1928).

FELLER, ABRAHAM HOWARD. *Some Observations on the Calvo Clause.* 27 AMERICAN JOURNAL OF INTERNATIONAL LAW 461 (1933).

FITZMAURICE, G. G. *The Meaning of the Term "Denial of Justice."* 13 BRITISH YEARBOOK OF INTERNATIONAL LAW 93 (1932).

FRALEIGH, ARNOLD. *The United States–Japanese Property Commission.* 56 AMERICAN JOURNAL OF INTERNATIONAL LAW 407 (1962).

FREEMAN, ALWYN V. *Recent Aspects of the Calvo Doctrine and the Challenge to International Law.* 40 AMERICAN JOURNAL OF INTERNATIONAL LAW 121 (1946).

GARCIA-AMADOR, F. V. *State Responsibility in the Light of the New Trends of International Law.* 49 AMERICAN JOURNAL OF INTERNATIONAL LAW 339 (1955).

BIBLIOGRAPHY

GARCIA-MORA, MANUEL R. *The Calvo Clause in Latin American Constitutions and International Law.* 33 MARQUETTE LAW REVIEW 205 (1950).

GARDNER, RICHARD N. *International Measures for the Promotion and Protection of Foreign Investment.* 9 JOURNAL OF PUBLIC LAW 176 (1960).

GARNER, JAMES W. *Decisions of the German-American Mixed Claims Commission.* 1924 BRITISH YEARBOOK OF INTERNATIONAL LAW 222.

GILLILLAND, WHITNEY. *The Foreign Claims Settlement Commission.* 11 AMERICAN BAR ASSOCIATION SECTION OF INTERNATIONAL AND COMPARATIVE LAW BULLETIN NO. 2 (1958).

GOEBEL, JR., JULIAN. *The International Responsibility for Injuries Sustained by Aliens on Account of Mob Violence, Insurrections, and Civil Wars.* 8 AMERICAN JOURNAL OF INTERNATIONAL LAW 802 (1914).

GOODMAN, RICHARD M. *Claims Involving American Life and Property Abroad under the Federal Foreign Claims Act.* 37 UNIVERSITY OF DETROIT LAW JOURNAL 617 (1960).

GRAVING, RICHARD J. *Shareholder Claims Against Cuba.* 48 AMERICAN BAR ASSOCIATION JOURNAL 226, 335 (1962).

GUTTERIDGE, JOYCE. *Expropriation and Nationalisation in Hungary, Bulgaria, and Roumania.* 1 INTERNATIONAL AND COMPARATIVE LAW QUARTERLY 14 (1952).

HACKWORTH, GREEN HAYWOOD. *The Responsibility of States for Damages Caused in Their Territory to the Person or Property of Foreigners.* 24 AMERICAN JOURNAL OF INTERNATIONAL LAW 500 (1930).

HANNA, JOHN. *Legal Liability for War Damages.* 43 MICHIGAN LAW REVIEW 1057 (1945).

———. *Nationality and War Claims.* 45 COLUMBIA LAW REVIEW 301 (1945).

HERMAN, SAMUEL. *War Damage and Nationalization in Eastern Europe.* 16 LAW AND CONTEMPORARY PROBLEMS 498 (1951).

HERSHEY, AMOS S. *The Calvo and Drago Doctrines.* 1 AMERICAN JOURNAL OF INTERNATIONAL LAW 26 (1907).

HERZ, JOHN H. *Expropriation of Foreign Property.* 35 AMERICAN JOURNAL OF INTERNATIONAL LAW 243 (1941).

HUNT, BERT L. *The United States–Panama General Claims Commission.* 28 AMERICAN JOURNAL OF INTERNATIONAL LAW 61 (1934).

——. *Work of General Claims Commission United States and Mexico.* 3 FEDERAL BAR JOURNAL 83 (1937).

HURST, CECIL J. B. *Nationality of Claims.* 1926 BRITISH YEARBOOK OF INTERNATIONAL LAW 163.

HYDE, CHARLES CHENEY. *Compensation for Expropriation.* 33 AMERICAN JOURNAL OF INTERNATIONAL LAW 108 (1939).

——. *Concerning Attempts by Contract to Restrict Interposition.* 21 AMERICAN JOURNAL OF INTERNATIONAL LAW 298 (1927).

——. *Confiscatory Expropriation.* 32 AMERICAN JOURNAL OF INTERNATIONAL LAW 759 (1938).

HYDE, JAMES N. *Permanent Sovereignty Over Natural Wealth and Resources.* 50 AMERICAN JOURNAL OF INTERNATIONAL LAW 854 (1956).

JESSUP, PHILIP C. *Responsibility of States for Injuries to Individuals.* 46 COLUMBIA LAW REVIEW 903 (1946).

——. *The Litvinov Assignment and the Pink Case.* 36 AMERICAN JOURNAL OF INTERNATIONAL LAW 282 (1942).

JONES, J. MERVYN. *Claims on Behalf of Nationals Who Are Shareholders in Foreign Companies.* 26 BRITISH YEARBOOK OF INTERNATIONAL LAW 225 (1949).

KAECKENBEECK, G. *The Protection of Vested Rights in International Law.* 17 BRITISH YEARBOOK OF INTERNATIONAL LAW 1 (1936).

KANE, ALBERT E. *Some Unsolved Problems Regarding War Damage Claims Under Article 78 of the Treaty of Peace With Italy.* 45 AMERICAN JOURNAL OF INTERNATIONAL LAW 357 (1951).

KISSAM, LEO T. *Sovereign Expropriation of Property and Abrogation of Concession Contracts.* 28 FORDHAM LAW REVIEW 177 (1959).

KNIGHT, GEORGE STEPHENS. *International Claims and Their Preparation.* 3 FEDERAL BAR JOURNAL 205, 282 (1938).

KOESSLER, MAXIMILIAN. *Government Espousal of Private Claims Be-

fore International Tribunals. 13 UNIVERSITY OF CHICAGO LAW RE-VIEW 180 (1946).

KUHN, ARTHUR K. *Nationalization of Foreign-Owned Property in its Impact on International Law.* 45 AMERICAN JOURNAL OF INTERNATIONAL LAW 709 (1951).

KUNZ, JOSEF L. *The Mexican Expropriations.* 17 NEW YORK UNIVERSITY LAW QUARTERLY REVIEW 327 (1940).

LAMBIE, MARGARET. *Presumptions of Cessation of Citizenship: Its Effect on International Claims.* 24 AMERICAN JOURNAL OF INTERNATIONAL LAW 264 (1930).

LARSON, ARTHUR. *Recipient's Rights Under an International Investment Code.* 9 JOURNAL OF PUBLIC LAW 173 (1960).

LEACH, EDMOND K. *Sovereign Expropriation of Property and Abrogation of Concession Contracts.* 28 FORDHAM LAW REVIEW 177 (1959).

LIPSTEIN, K. *The Place of the Calvo Clause in International Law.* 22 BRITISH YEARBOOK OF INTERNATIONAL LAW 130 (1945).

LISSITZYN, OLIVER J. *The Meaning of the Term Denial of Justice in International Law.* 30 AMERICAN JOURNAL OF INTERNATIONAL LAW 632 (1936).

MANN, F. A. *State Contracts and State Responsibility.* 54 AMERICAN JOURNAL OF INTERNATIONAL LAW 572 (1960).

————. *The Law Governing State Contracts.* 21 BRITISH YEARBOOK OF INTERNATIONAL LAW 11 (1944).

MASON, MALCOLM S. *Relationship of Vested Assets to War Claims.* 16 LAW AND CONTEMPORARY PROBLEMS 395 (1951).

MCKERNAN, LOUIS W. *Special Mexican Claims.* 32 AMERICAN JOURNAL OF INTERNATIONAL LAW 457 (1938).

MERON, THEODOR. *The Incidence of the Rule of Exhaustion of Local Remedies.* 35 BRITISH YEARBOOK OF INTERNATIONAL LAW 83 (1959).

METZGER, STANLEY D. *Multilateral Conventions for the Protection of Private Foreign Investment.* 9 JOURNAL OF PUBLIC LAW 133 (1960).

MILLER, ARTHUR S. *Protection of Private Foreign Investment by Multilateral Convention.* 53 AMERICAN JOURNAL OF INTERNATIONAL LAW 341 (1959).

MORGAN, MARSHALL. *The Work of the Mixed Claims Commission, United States and Germany.* 4 TEXAS LAW REVIEW 399 (1926).

MYERS, DENYS P. (Editor). *Contemporary Practice of the United States Relating to International Law.* 53 AMERICAN JOURNAL OF INTERNATIONAL LAW 896 (1959).

NIELSEN, FREDERICK KENELM. *Progress in Settlement of International Disputes by Judicial Methods.* 16 AMERICAN BAR ASSOCIATION JOURNAL 229 (1930).

———. *Some Vexatious Questions Relating to Nationality.* 20 COLUMBIA LAW REVIEW 840 (1920).

NOTE. *Expropriation of Alien Property.* 109 UNIVERSITY OF PENNSYLVANIA LAW REVIEW 245 (1960).

NOTE. *Foreign Seizure of Investments: Remedies and Protection.* 12 STANFORD LAW REVIEW 606 (1960).

NOTE. *Private Interests in Claims Against Foreign States.* 42 HARVARD LAW REVIEW 930 (1929).

NOTE. *Validity of an Award by Mixed Claims Commission Not a Judicial Question.* 27 VIRGINIA LAW REVIEW 394 (1941).

NUSSBAUM, ARTHUR. *The Arbitration Between the Lena Goldfields, Ltd. and the Soviet Government.* 36 CORNELL LAW QUARTERLY 31 (1950).

OLIVER, COVEY T. *Executive Agreements and Emanations from the Fifth Amendment.* 49 AMERICAN JOURNAL OF INTERNATIONAL LAW 362 (1955).

OLMSTEAD, CECIL J. *Nationalization of Foreign Property Interests, Particularly Those Subject to Agreements with the State.* 32 NEW YORK UNIVERSITY LAW REVIEW 1122 (1957).

———. *Economic Development Agreements Part II: Agreements Between States and Aliens; Choice of Law and Remedy.* 49 CALIFORNIA LAW REVIEW 504 (1961).

ORFIELD, LESTER B. *Equity as a Concept of International Law.* 18 KENTUCKY LAW JOURNAL 31, 116 (1929–1930).

———. *The Legal Effects of Dual Nationality.* 17 GEORGE WASHINGTON LAW REVIEW 427 (1949).

PESELJ, BRANKO M. *The Rule of the Nationality of Claimant, Due*

Process of Law and the United States Congress. 53 AMERICAN JOURNAL OF INTERNATIONAL LAW 144 (1959).

PUENTE, J. IRIZARRY Y. *The Concept of "Denial of Justice" in Latin America.* 43 MICHIGAN LAW REVIEW 383 (1944).

RALSTON, JACKSON H. *International Awards.* 15 VIRGINIA LAW REVIEW 1 (1928).

RAY, JR., GEORGE W. *Law Governing Contracts Between States and Foreign Nationals,* IN 2 INSTITUTE ON PRIVATE INVESTMENTS ABROAD 5 (1960).

RE, EDWARD DOMENIC. *Nationalization and Investment of Capital Abroad.* 42 GEORGETOWN LAW JOURNAL 44 (1953).

————. *The Nationalization of Foreign-Owned Property.* 36 MINNESOTA LAW REVIEW 323 (1952).

————. *Foreign Claims Settlement Commission of the United States,* IN NEW YORK STATE BAR ASSOCIATION, REPORT OF COMMITTEE ON INTERNATIONAL LAW 19 (1961).

————. *The Foreign Claims Settlement Commission and International Claims.* 13 SYRACUSE LAW REVIEW 516 (1962).

RICE, JR., WILLIAM GORHAM. *State Responsibility for Failure to Vindicate the Public Peace.* 28 AMERICAN JOURNAL OF INTERNATIONAL LAW 246 (1934).

RODE, ZVONKO R. *Dual Nationals and the Doctrine of Dominant Nationality.* 53 AMERICAN JOURNAL OF INTERNATIONAL LAW 139 (1959).

————. *The American-Polish Claims Agreement of 1960.* 55 AMERICAN JOURNAL OF INTERNATIONAL LAW 452 (1961).

————. *The International Claims Commission of the United States.* 47 AMERICAN JOURNAL OF INTERNATIONAL LAW 615 (1953).

ROOT, ELIHU. *The Basis of Protection to Citizens Residing Abroad.* 4 AMERICAN JOURNAL OF INTERNATIONAL LAW 517 (1910).

ROY, S. N. GUHA. *Is the Law of Responsibility of States for Injuries to Aliens a Part of Universal International Law?* 55 AMERICAN JOURNAL OF INTERNATIONAL LAW 863 (1961).

RUBIN, SEYMOUR. *Nationalization and Compensation: A Comparative Approach.* 17 UNIVERSITY OF CHICAGO LAW REVIEW 458 (1951).

————. *The Almost-Forgotten Claimant: American Citizens' Property Rights Violated.* 40 AMERICAN BAR ASSOCIATION JOURNAL 961 (1954).

SCHACHTER, OSCAR. *Private Foreign Investment and International Organization.* 45 CORNELL LAW QUARTERLY 415 (1960).

SCHWARZENBERGER, GEORG. *The Abs-Shawcross Draft Convention on Investments Abroad: A Critical Commentary.* 9 JOURNAL OF PUBLIC LAW 147 (1960).

SCHWEBEL, STEPHEN M. *International Protection of Contractual Arrangements.* 53 AMERICAN SOCIETY OF INTERNATIONAL LAW PROCEEDINGS 266 (1959).

SEIDEL-HOHENVELDERN, IGNAZ. *Communist Theories on Confiscation and Expropriation.* 7 AMERICAN JOURNAL OF COMPARATIVE LAW 541 (1958).

————. *General Principles of Law as Applied by the Conciliation Commissions Established Under the Peace Treaty With Italy of 1947.* 53 AMERICAN JOURNAL OF INTERNATIONAL LAW 853 (1959).

————. *The Abs-Shawcross Draft Convention to Protect Private Foreign Investment: Comments on the Round Table.* 10 JOURNAL OF PUBLIC LAW 100 (1961).

SILVANIE, HAIG. *Responsibility of States for Acts of Insurgent Governments.* 33 AMERICAN JOURNAL OF INTERNATIONAL LAW 78 (1939).

SINCLAIR, I. M. *Nationality of Claims: British Practice.* 27 BRITISH YEARBOOK OF INTERNATIONAL LAW 125 (1950).

SIPKOV, IVAN. *Postwar Nationalizations and Alien Property in Bulgaria.* 52 AMERICAN JOURNAL OF INTERNATIONAL LAW 469 (1958).

SOMMERICH, OTTO B. *Italy: Foreign Expropriation and Public Order.* 5 AMERICAN JOURNAL OF COMPARATIVE LAW 641 (1956).

SPIEGEL, HANS W. *Origin and Development of Denial of Justice.* 32 AMERICAN JOURNAL OF INTERNATIONAL LAW 63 (1938).

STARKE, J. G. *Imputability in International Delinquencies.* 19 BRITISH YEARBOOK OF INTERNATIONAL LAW 104 (1938).

SUMMERS, LIONEL MORGAN. *The Calvo Clause.* 19 VIRGINIA LAW REVIEW 459 (1933).

BIBLIOGRAPHY

————. *The United States–Japanese Property Commission.* 56 AMERICAN JOURNAL OF INTERNATIONAL LAW 407 (1962).

SURREY, WALTER STERLING. *Problems of the Italian Peace Treaty: Analysis of Claims Provisions and Description of Enforcement.* 16 LAW AND CONTEMPORARY PROBLEMS 435 (1951).

TATE, JACK B. *International Reclamations and the Peace Settlements.* 43 AMERICAN SOCIETY OF INTERNATIONAL LAW PROCEEDINGS 27 (1949).

THOMAS, JR., A. J. *Protection of Property of Citizens Abroad,* IN 1 INSTITUTE ON PRIVATE INVESTMENTS ABROAD 417 (1959).

TOELLE, J. H. *The Court of Claims: Its Jurisdiction and Principal Decisions Bearing on International Law.* 24 MICHIGAN LAW REVIEW 675 (1926).

TURLINGTON, EDGAR. *Work of the Special Claims Commission United States and Mexico.* 3 FEDERAL BAR JOURNAL 23 (1937).

UJLAKI, NICHOLAS. *Compensation for the Nationalization of American-Owned Property in Bulgaria, Hungary and Rumania.* 1 NEW YORK LAW FORUM 265 (1955).

WADMOND, LOWELL C. *The Judicial Protection of Property Abroad.* 16 BUSINESS LAWYER 688 (1961).

WETTER, J. GILLIS. *Diplomatic Assistance to Private Investment.* 29 UNIVERSITY OF CHICAGO LAW REVIEW 275 (1962).

WILLIAMS, JOHN FISCHER. *International Law and the Property of Aliens.* 1928 BRITISH YEARBOOK OF INTERNATIONAL LAW 1.

WILSON, ROBERT R. *Property-Protection Provisions in United States Commercial Treaties.* 45 AMERICAN JOURNAL OF INTERNATIONAL LAW 83 (1951).

————. *Some Aspects of the Jurisprudence of National Claims Commissions.* 36 AMERICAN JOURNAL OF INTERNATIONAL LAW 56 (1942).

WOOLSLEY, LESTER H. *The Expropriation of Oil Properties by Mexico.* 32 AMERICAN JOURNAL OF INTERNATIONAL LAW 519 (1938).

————. *The Settlement of Claims Between the United States and Mexico.* 30 AMERICAN JOURNAL OF INTERNATIONAL LAW 99 (1936).

WORTLEY, B. A. *Expropriation in International Law*, IN 33 TRANSACTIONS OF THE GROTIUS SOCIETY 25 (1948).

———. *Observations on the Public and Private International Law Relating to Expropriation*. 5 AMERICAN JOURNAL OF COMPARATIVE LAW 577 (1956).

———. *The Protection of Property Situated Abroad*. 35 TULANE LAW REVIEW 739 (1961).

WRIGHT, QUINCY. *War Claims: What of the Future?* 16 LAW AND CONTEMPORARY PROBLEMS 543 (1951).

YNTEMA, HESSEL E. *The Treaties with Germany and Compensation for War Damages*. 23 COLUMBIA LAW REVIEW 511 (1923).

YOUNG, RICHARD. *Remedies of Private Claimants Against Foreign States*, IN 3 INSTITUTE ON PRIVATE INVESTMENT ABROAD 45 (1961).

Index

Foreign Claims Commission (*cont.*)
subsidiary corporation, 46; examination of witnesses, 53; "judicial" notice, 57; attitude toward secondary evidence, 59, 78–80; inspections of property, 61; aid in procuring evidence, 61, 75; use of interrogatories, 61; employment of expert appraisers, 77–78; gathers own evidence, 79, 87; reduction of award for insufficient evidence, 45, 79–80, 83n, 111; power to issue subpoenas and order depositions taken, 106–107; burden of proof, 109; newly discovered evidence, 112
—Views on: continuity of nationality rule, 9–11; date of property taking, 58

Foreign law. *See* Local law
Foreign trade and investment, 2–3

German Claims Act, 2
Germany, 2, 59, 61, 65, 94
Good offices, 99, 100
Guardians. *See* Claimants

Heirs. *See* Claimants
Hungary, 10, 19, 57, 58, 63, 66

Immigration and Naturalization Service, 32, 34–35
Insurers. *See* Claimants
International claims: amount paid to Americans, 1; possible increase in number, 2–3; as theoretically accruing to states, 7, 40, 92; ownership, 8–10; ways of handling, 88
International Claims Commission, 4, 94
International claims commissions, 115–116
International Claims Settlement Act, 10–11
International Court of Justice, 96
International law: paucity of remedies, 3; departures from usual nationality rule, 10–11; as standard for testing official acts, 53; violations, 54, 56–65 *passim;* acts if lesser officials not imputed to country, 55; compensability of war claims, 66;

non-discriminatory imposition of foreign exchange controls no basis for claim, 86–87; use of by Legal Adviser's Office to judge claims, 90, 92; possible influence of political procedures on law, 101–102
International politics: effect on claims, 90, 92, 98–99, 100, 101
Interstate claims, 5n
Intervention. *See* Political intervention
Italy, 6, 19, 35, 44, 63, 66, 70, 74

Japan, 6, 28, 44
Joint claims, 41–42
Judicial review of awards, 33–34, 51n, 103, 112–115

Laches, 91–92
Legal Adviser's Office. *See* Department of State
Legatees. *See* Claimants
Local law: nationality as a matter of, 9; of inheritance, 23, 44–45; of transferability of ownership, 44, 46; violation of as defense to claim, 91
Lump sum settlements, 16, 55, 98, 101–102, 103, 112–115 *passim*

Mediation, 99, 100
Mexico, 56
Minors. *See* Claimants
Mixed claims commissions, 115–116
Mortgagees. *See* Claimants
Municipal law. *See* Local law

Nationality: in general, 8–17 *passim;* definition, 8n; matter of municipal law, 9; method of acquisition, 9; continuity of nationality rule, 9–12, 23–24, 25, 31–32, 35, 40–41, 49–50; of citizens nationalized after accrual of claim, 11, 92n, 101; possible loss of, 12, 35, 92; dual, 12–13; effect of Calvo Clause, 13–14; effect on protection of partnerships, 14–15, 36–38; effect on protection of corporations, 15–17, 38–39; effect on protection of stockholders, 17–20; of administrator of claimant's estate,

Colophon

INTERNATIONAL CLAIMS: *Their Preparation and Presentation* has been set in 11 point
Linotype Janson, leaded 3 points, printed on 60
pound Glatfelter Antique Book, and bound in
Columbia Milbank Linen over 80 point binder's
board by the Vail-Ballou Press, Inc.

SIU
PRESS